MW00681197

HONG KONG

PASSPORT BOOKS

Trade Imprint of National Textbook Company
Lincolnwood, Illinois U.S.A.

Published by Passport Books in conjunction
with China Guides Series Ltd.

Contents

The spelling of Chinese names in this guide follows the Wade-Giles system prevalent in Hong Kong and not the pinyin system now used in Mainland China.

All prices quoted are in Hong Kong dollars.

Hong Kong, China

An Introduction by May Holdsworth

Hong Kong seems positively to invite cliché definitions: the pearl in the dragon's mouth, the duty-free shopping paradise, the glittering epitome of *laisse faire* capitalism standing cheek-by-jowl with the world's largest Communist state . . . . . All these descriptions do serve, to some extent, to encapsulate the paradoxes of the territory's singular political status and diversity of lifestyles. But perhaps the essence of Hong Kong resides in the very anomaly of its existence.

Hong Kong was always regarded as a peculiar place. To begin with, its geography and history are remarkable. Situated on the coast of China's Guangdong Province, at the mouth of the Pearl River, the Crown Colony is a patchwork consisting of the island of Hong Kong, the part of the Kowloon peninsula south of Boundary Street, the hinterland beyond up to the border with China (known as the New Territories), and 235 islands, the most developed ones being Lantau, Lamma and Cheung Chau. About 130 kilometres to the northwest is the Chinese city of Guangzhou (Canton), and approximately 65 kilometres to the west across the estuary is the Portuguese enclave of Macau.

The total land area of Hong Kong is about 1046 square kilometres — an approximation because small bits of land are occasionally added through reclamation. Its population of 5.5 million occupies one of the most densely inhabited urban centres in the world. The natural beauty of its landscape is no longer very visible. Many of those wild mountain ranges, so reminiscent — it was said by early colonisers — of the Scottish Highlands, have been gouged out to make way for new towns and buildings. But on an early autumn morning, in a few remaining isolated spots, glimpses of the purple hillsides sloping down towards sparkling bays can still take one's breath away.

Under the 1842 Treaty of Nanking, which concluded the First Opium War between China and Great Britain, Hong Kong Island was ceded in perpetuity to Britain. The Treaties of Tientsin and Peking provided in 1860 for the cession — also in perpetuity — of the Kowloon peninsula and Stonecutter's Island in the harbour. Later, to secure the colony against outside attack, Britain demanded and acquired a 99-year lease on the 365 square mile New Territories and most of the adjacent islands from 1 July 1898. These pacts came to be known as the 'Unequal Treaties'. Thus by 'an accident of history', as both Britain and China now choose to sum up the bizarre proceedings, Hong Kong is still a British colony, even though colonialism has long been in retreat everywhere else. In fact, until only recently, the thrust of decolonisation has been conspicuously absent in Hong Kong, where representative institutions and democratic forms have been slow in emerging.

The questions and anxieties surrounding the New Territories lease were finally resolved by the Joint Declaration signed by the British and Chinese governments on 19 December 1984. Only time will reveal the agonising behind the scenes that led to the final settlement. The negotiators had, after all, to wrestle with a very peculiar historical transaction — a lease on which, strictly speaking, the tenant has never paid any rent, and which the landlord since 1949 has never recognised anyway. Under the Sino-British agreement, then, China resumes the exercise of sovereignty on 1 July 1997 over all of Hong Kong, which will become a Special Administrative Region under the authority of the Chinese central government. As Hong Kong, China — the name under which it will trade and enter into economic and cultural agreements with other states — it will effectively be given the right of internal self-government. China's leaders have also guaranteed the Region's economic, social and legal autonomy for a further 50 years, rationalising the seemingly incongruous arrangement by their self-proclaimed imaginative and far-sighted 'One Country, Two Systems' policy. Hong Kong will become the subject of a unique political experiment. And upon the successful outcome of this experiment may depend the reunification of the less tractable Taiwan, on which China has long set her sights.

China's reasons for preserving Hong Kong's systems and way of life after 1997 are pragmatic. Peking is estimated to earn some 40% of its total foreign exchange receipts in Hong Kong, which also provides it with a captive market for Chinese foodstuffs, basic consumer goods and fresh water. The agencies through which this commercial traffic is conducted include the 13 Chinese-controlled banks in the colony, headed by a branch of the Bank of China, a chain of department stores, several investment companies, and a huge trading corporation, China Resources Company Limited.

Hong Kong is equally important in serving as the main communications link between China and the outside world, particularly her suppliers of technology. It is infinitely easier for both sides to do business through a technically proficient intermediary, who speaks Cantonese and English fluently, and who has perhaps also boned up on his Putonghua (Mandarin). Hong Kong itself has considerable reserves of expertise in finance, management, manufacturing and technical education.

At one time Hong Kong's most prized asset was its deep natural harbour. The extensive port facilities on the Kowloon peninsula are indeed among the finest in the world, but today no one would dispute that the vital factor in Hong Kong's economic success is its diligent and adaptable work force, manning a light industrial base that is nothing if not flexible. Local manufacturers are remarkably adept at responding to market fads. A toy factory can flood the world with model spaceships one year and Cabbage Patch dolls the next. Garment manufactures — under pressure from protectionist restrictions in export markets — were able to switch from cheap jeans to sophisticated silk fashions without threat of strikes or work-to-rule.

This flexibility in industry or business is a visible demonstration of the inherent Hong Kong mentality — a frenetic dedication to the here and now. Hitherto Hong Kong people could hardly have afforded to plan for the long term. A majority of the predominantly (98%) Chinese population consists of refugees and children of refugees. Those born in Hong Kong have acquired British nationality of sorts but, since recent British immigration legislation, it is not the kind of citizenship that automatically confers right of abode in the United Kingdom. Coupled with the 1997 deadline, this 'statelessness' had created an urgent, aggressive opportunism. Making a fast buck is still patently possible, as borne out by the fortunes amassed spectacularly in one generation by local tycoons. Some of the new rich have, of course, long secured their boltholes in the capitalist West: passports in exchange for investments, or residence qualifications through children studying and then settling abroad. Nevertheless, with the venturesome shrewdness characteristic of Hong Kong entrepreneurs, they are joining the China trade stampede with cautious enthusiasm. Bourgeois attitudes notwithstanding, they want to be seen as friends of China. Yet it is not just for mercenary reasons that they are investing in the motherland. There is a genuine affinity with their cousins across the border, a stirring of dormant patriotism, a philanthropic wish to benefit the villages of their ancestors. The Chinese county and provincial authorities, for their part, are only too eager to extend the gesture of amity, when sentiment is given tangible expression by way of donations and investment. It remains to be seen how the rest of Hong Kong's population, with less cash and no clout, will adjust to a less uncertain future.

Alongside are the expatriates — the taipans of the hongs (British trading houses), the administrators who will eventually 'go home', the businessmen of all nationalities. The foreign community, though tiny in absolute numbers, is a palpable presence. Its members hold many of the top jobs and some of them enjoy a lifestyle undreamed of in their own countries. There are still clubs where the admission of local Chinese as members is discreetly, but nevertheless effectively, restricted. One wonders how these bastions of privilege will survive the onslaught of a swarm of cadres.

It was the expatriates' tenure in the colony that initially gave it a cosmopolitan flavour, one which is now increasingly dominated by Americans, rather than by the British. The United States has traditionally been the Eldorado of Chinese refugees, who have sent their sons and daughters there in droves: to pursue higher education, better opportunities or Green Cards. In the New York-style bars of Hong Kong's entertainment quarter, in boardrooms and banks, these US-returned graduates, their American drawls grafted onto native Cantonese accents, are making an impact. They may well become, Peking permitting, Hong Kong's future ruling elite. To nurture a new generation of leaders, the Government is rushing to localise the civil service; and the first move towards representative democracy, with direct elections by 1988, was made within months of the Sino-British agreement.

Among the foreign businessmen, the Americans and Japanese are the most bullish about Hong Kong's future. They account for the largest proportion of overseas investment, seeing the territory as a financial launching pad for the vast China market and a relatively cheap high-tech manufacturing base. Edging close as a major trading partner is China herself, whose commerce with Hong Kong has increased dramatically in the last two years. Even more striking is Hong Kong's resumption of its traditional role as entrepôt for Chinese goods. Now it not only buys more from the mainland, but re-exports into China have climbed steeply as well. This interdependent relationship can only draw Hong Kong closer to China.

The more international investment Hong Kong can attract, the harder it will become for China to interfere in its financial activities and the better it will be for Hong Kong's future. Moreover, Hong Kong needs to stay ahead of China technologically and industrially at least until 2047, by which time, it is hoped, China will have arrived at an irreversible stage in her own economic reforms. All supposing, of course, that China's present political stability remains undisrupted by any radical swings in ideology. Pessimists have only to point to China's recent political upheavals to justify their sense of unease.

Hong Kong is walking a tightrope, and in the run-up to 1997 it will have to tread the capitalist path with circumspection. At the moment it is indispensable to China's modernisation. For how long will it remain so?

Arriving in Hong Kong

The Airport Few of the world's airports can rival the spectacular approach to Hong Kong's Kai Tak Airport. By day a glimpse of the many islands scattered over the South China Sea is followed by a breath-taking close-up of tightly packed high-rise buildings set against a mountainous backdrop. By night there is an equally impressive spectacle of banks of light rising steeply up the slopes of Hong Kong Island. On a southwesterly flight path, planes approach over the narrow channel between the islands of Lantau and Lamma and turn sharply at Beacon Hill before dropping over the densely-populated Kowloon area. From the east, planes fly by the easterly tip of Hong Kong Island and descend over water onto the 11,130 feet runway built out into Kowloon Bay.

Like many of Hong Kong's public facilities, Kai Tak has barely been able to keep up with the expanding numbers of users. Economy-class arrivals should expect a minimum of half an hour to come through customs and immigration which might extend well beyond an hour at peak times.

The terminal building, with its busy concourses and minimum of seating, is designed for efficient passenger handling. In the pre-departure section a vast graceless restaurant serves adequate Chinese or western meals and snacks. There are no public announcements for flight departures anywhere in the airport — passengers must keep an eye on the computerized departure boards. An airport tax of $120 is charged when leaving Hong Kong.

For arriving passengers there are helpful information counters run by the Hong Kong Tourist Association (HKTA), the Hong Kong Hotels Association (which will book rooms for you), and the Hong Kong Association of Travel Agents.

Transport from the Airport There are ordinary taxis (make sure the driver uses the meter) or a fleet of white Mercedes (more readily available than taxis, but more expensive) which can be hired in the arrivals hall. Two regular airport bus services run between the airport and Tsimshatsui or Central. No 201 goes along Nathan Road past or close to most Tsimshatsui hotels ($2.50 from 8am-10.30pm) and no. 200 goes to Hong Kong Island past the Plaza, Excelsior and Cathay Hotels in Causeway Bay, along Hennessy Road to the Furama, Mandarin and Hilton in Central ($4.00 from 7.31am-11.18pm). Many hotels have their own airport buses. Contact a hotel representative outside the customs hall, or ask at the Hong Kong Hotels Association desk.

Although Kai Tak is very near the city centre, allow at least half an hour to get to the airport from Tsimshatsui and an hour from Central during morning and evening rush hours. At other times it takes about 20 minutes from either area.

In addition to Kai Tak, an international airport is planned for Shenzhen, just across the border in China. This facility, the first phase of which is expected to be completed in 1988, will serve the entire South China coast including Hong Kong.

Visas Visa requirements differ, depending upon nationality. Visitors from most countries can enter Hong Kong without a visa for periods which vary from 7 days to 6 months. US citizens can stay for a month without a visa, while Commonwealth citizens can stay up to 3 months. Visitors from western European countries fall either into the 3-month or 1-month category. UK citizens with passports issued in Britain do not need visas at all — when they first arrive a stay of 6 months is normally granted, and an extension is usually easily obtained.

All visitors must of course hold valid travel documents, and should be able to show they have enough funds to cover their stay in Hong Kong, and an onward, or return, ticket.

Customs As a free trade centre, Hong Kong allows most items to enter duty free. The only dutiable items are tobacco, alcohol and petroleum products. There are duty-free allowances of 200 cigarettes, 50 cigars, or ½lb of tobacco; one quart of alcohol; perfume in reasonable quantities. Firearms (that is, personal property such as rifles and revolvers) must be declared and handed into custody until departure.

Vaccinations No vaccinations are required unless you have been in a cholera or smallpox infected area within the preceding 14 days.

Climate and Clothing

Hong Kong has a climate with distinct seasons. A long, hot and humid summer with heavy rain contrasts with a drier and cooler (occasionally chilly) winter. There are short autumn and spring seasons.

By far the most pleasant weather is during autumn and early winter, from October to the end of December. Skies are clear and blue, the humidity lower (around 70%) and there is little rain. Temperatures during the day reach the mid 20°Cs and rarely fall below 10°C in the evening.

January and February are the coldest months — temperatures as low as 0°C have been recorded, although the average is around 16°C. In February the humidity begins to rise again and March and April are usually damp and depressing, with low clouds and mist obscuring even the lower hills, and little sunshine and increasingly higher temperatures. This is the season when residents complain of mildewed leather, soggy newspapers and walls running with condensation.

By May summer has begun. For the next four months temperatures usually reach 30°C-32°C every day, without dropping conspicuously at night. Three quarters of the annual rainfall occurs in this period, often in heavy outbursts, but there is plenty of hot sun too — a average of 240 hours in June. Humidity is 90% or more. This is also the season for typhoons, (tropical storms which have developed winds of hurricane force). There are happily few direct hits, but even from a hundred miles away, a typhoon can do considerable damage. The Royal Observatory, with its new satellite ground station, can provide extremely accurate information on the whereabouts of the cyclone centre and the maximum wind speeds. The public are given plenty of warning by the Observatory's series of signals. (These are flags hoisted at various points throughout the colony and announced at frequent intervals on television and radio.) Number 1 warns that a tropical storm is within 400 nautical miles of Hong Kong. Number 3 means that the storm is approaching Hong Kong and winds of at least 22 knots which may gust to 60 knots may be expected within 12 hours. At this point boats go into typhoon shelters and ferries to outlying islands may be cancelled. At Number 8 (usually only hoisted once or twice a year) all offices must by law close to allow workers home before public transport stops. Shops shut and just about everything comes to a standstill. Number 10 (a rare occurrence) indicates that a typhoon is in town with hurricane winds of 64 knots or more.

What to Wear Visitors usually find the Hong Kong Chinese well dressed and fashion conscious. Air-conditioning is just about universal in hotels, restaurants and the larger shops in central areas, nonetheless, lightweight clothes are essential for summer. Men can wear light trousers and shirts on most occasions during summer, although jackets and ties are advisable for some business appointments and are mandatory in a few smart restaurants. They are also required in some hotel bars such as the Mandarin's Captain's Bar in the evening. For winter (particularly January and February) bring some warm clothes — sweaters, jackets and a light overcoat.

Money

Currency As the financial centre of Asia, Hong Kong has over 110 licensed banks from 17 countries. Bank of America, Citibank, Chase Manhattan, Banque Nationale de Paris, Barclays International, Bank of Tokyo — to name a few — all have several branches, and a comprehensive network of Chinese banks as well as the Bank of China covers the territory. Banking hours are from 9.30 or 10am to 3pm, with some banks opening also 4-6pm.

There is no Central Bank in Hong Kong. The local Hongkong and Shanghai Banking Corporation — established in 1864 by Hong Kong-based merchants — and the London-based Chartered Bank issue the colony's banknotes. They are in denominations of $1000, $500, $100, $50 and

$10; in addition there are $5, $2, $1, 50 cents, 20 cents and 10 cents coins. Hong Kong currency can be freely imported or exported.

Exchange Currencies and travellers cheques can be changed at any bank or at hotels (where the rate tends to be less favourable) and at the many money changers in the business district, such as Lark International Finance Ltd., with branches in Swire House and Shell House. Most shops frequently by tourists will also accept payment in hard foreign currencies. As a rough guide the exchange rates for major currencies in Sumer 1985 are:

US$1	HK$7.75	1DM	HK$2.52
Can$1	HK$5.66	1FF	HK$0.82
A$1	HK$5.07	1SW Krona	HK$3.00
£1	HK$9.85	1 Dutch Guilder	HK$2.24

Credit cards Credit cards are widely accepted although shops tend to offer a discount for cash.

Tipping Restaurants, bars and hotels generally add a 10% service charge to bills, but it is customary to leave small change for the waiters. For short trips within the city taxi drivers do not expect a tip, elsewhere 5-10% is normal. The going rate for porters at the airport is $5 per piece of luggage. Hotel bell-boys expect $5 per bag carried. At barber shops and hairdressers a reasonable tip is 10% of the bill.

Language

For all its veneer of western sophistication, Hong Kong is unequivocally Chinese where language is concerned. The main Chinese dialect is Cantonese, which is as different from Mandarin, spoken throughout mainland China, as French is from Italian. Minority dialects include Shanghainese, Chiu Chow and Hakka.

Officially, English has equal status with Chinese, as reflected in bilingual road signs, public notices, and business and government documents. However, comprehension of English is limited among people you will encounter on public transport, and in shops and restaurants outside international hotels, or those catering to the local expatriate community. Taxi drivers can be relied on to recognize English names for obvious tourist destinations, but, if directed to anywhere off the beaten track, may take you round to the nearest police station for help, or simply ask you to try another taxi. The situation is complicated by the haphazard translations of street names. For example, 'Fa Yuen Do' literally means 'Garden Road', whereas 'Wan Hum Gai' is a transliteration based on the mispronunciation of 'Wyndham Street'. The adverturous tourist would be well advised to get a hotel receptionist to write out his intended destination in Chinese characters.

The Hong Kong Tourist Association

Tourism is big business in Hong Kong. More than 3.15 million visitors poured into the colony in 1984, spending some $13.7 billion on goods and services, an increase of almost 27% over the previous year. Responsibility for the smooth running of this important industry rests with the Hong Kong Tourist Association, an official government-sponsored body which coordinates the activities of the industry and advises on development.

The HKTA has won itself a favourable reputation amongst visitors for their efficient helpful service. If you need advice or information it is always worth trying the HKTA first. They man a telephone information service (tel. 5-244191 Monday-Friday and public holidays 8am-6pm; Saturday and Sunday 8am-1pm) and four information centres:

Star Ferry Concourse, Kowloon (by the ferry entrance) Monday-Friday and public holidays 8pm-6pm; Saturday and Sunday 8am-1pm

Government Publications Centre, General Post Office Building, Central, Hong Kong (just to the west of the Star Ferry entrance) Monday-Friday 9am-6pm; Saturday 9am-1pm

35th Floor, Connaught Centre, Central, Hong Kong (just to the west of the Star Ferry entrance) Monday-Friday 8am-6pm; Saturday 8am-1pm

Kai Tak Airport, Buffer Hall for arriving passengers, daily 10am-10pm

There are also representative offices in the USA, Europe and Australia. Cathay Pacific Airways represent the Association in other areas.

The HKTA publishes plenty of literature, including a useful tourist map and a series of leaflets, frequently updated, on shopping, hotels, beaches, museums, walks and other tourists topics. Their free pocket *Office Guidebook* is disappointingly padded out with advertisements, but the *Official Guide to the Best of Hong Kong Shopping* contains an indispensable list of all the HKTA-approved shops (some 1300 of them) and restaurants, together with a selected directory of services visitors may need, and some useful maps. They also publish a weekly newspaper *The Orient*, mostly useful for its practical information and 'What's On' column.

The familiar HKTA sign — a black junk enclosed in a circle — indicates that the member is nominally bound to 'maintain ethical standards' and to 'discourage malpractices contrary to the best interests of visitors'. The HKTA investigate any complaints against their members (which should be made by telephoning 5-244191 (Ext. 278) and can terminate anyone's membership if appropriate.

Telephones: Hong Kong's subscribers do not pay for local calls so phones are free in most hotel lobbies, restaurants and shops. A visitor need only ask to use one.

Getting around Hong Kong

The transport system of the world's most densely populated metropolis is, predictably, highly complex, and apparently in a state of perpetual modernization and expansion. Everything conspires to create a transport planner's nightmare: a fast growing population, the engineering problems caused by steep mountain slopes, a bedrock of decomposed granite and the ¾-mile stretch of water between the two main urban centres.

For the visitor, these problems have resulted in a delightfully wide range of forms of transport, which are well worth trying. However, in a territory where there are too many cars for the meagre 693 miles of road, there is a perennial problem of traffic congestion. Just about all forms of public transport are packed during rush hours (7.30-9.30am and 5-6.30pm). And on fine Sundays or public holidays ferries to outlying islands and all means of getting to the New Territories and to the beaches are equally crowded. If you want to be comfortable, you must simply avoid travelling at these times.

Taxis

Hong Kong taxis are cheap by international standards, and in most places can be easily hailed in the street except at particular times of day (around 4pm when drivers change over, and during rush hours). If you are caught in Central at these times, make for a taxi rank, such as the one at Star Ferry or just by the Mass Transit Railway's Admiralty station.

Taxi drivers are all licensed and the cars are metered. Flagfall is $5 for the first two kilometres, with 70 cents for every 0.27 kilometre thereafter. An additional $20 is charged if the cross-harbour tunnel is used, $2 for the Aberdeen tunnel. There is a second taxi service (green and white cars, as opposed to the urban red and silver ones) which is restricted to the rural areas in the New Territories. Flagfall for these taxis is $3.30.

Most drivers understand enough English to get you to the better-known destinations, although Kowloon drivers tend to be vague about Hong Kong Island, and vice versa. And if you do have a problem with an uncooperative driver, contact the HKTA or the police who will pass on your complaint to a special centre.

Ferries

Ferries are a major form of transport in Hong Kong. There are services from Hong Kong to all the major outlying islands, and others which link different points on both sides of Victoria Harbour [see the map on page 18]. There is a hover ferry service to Cheung Chau and to Tsuen Wan, as well as to Macau.

The best-known service is offered by the Star Ferry Company, whose ferries have been plying between Central and Tsimshatsui since the end of the last century. For atmosphere — and value for money — this seven-minute journey would be hard to beat anywhere in the world. Passengers pay at a turnstile — HK70 cents for first class (top deck), HK50 cents for second class (lower deck). The Star Ferry operates between 6.30am and 11.30pm. Passengers never have to wait more than a few minutes, except in the early morning and late at night on Sundays when departures are at 20-minutes intervals.

Sailing junk from Mainland China

Ferries to other islands, run by the Hong Kong and Yaumati Ferry Company, leave from the bustling, shabby Outlying Districts Ferry Pier in Central. Tickets are on sale about half an hour before departure — there are different ticket offices for each route. Queues form early at weekends (when many fares double), so it is best to travel midweek. Once on the boat, particularly if you sit out on the deluxe class open sun deck you will have a superb journey. Both Hong Kong Island and the mainland look magnificent from the sea, at night as well as daytime. And there is a wealth of other craft to look at — huge passenger liners, cargo vessels, jetfoils to Macau, fishing junks at work, and, if you are lucky, a red-sailed junk from mainland China.

Fares are $6 for deluxe class on a weekday to Lantau (one hour and fifteen minutes) and only $3 for the lower second class deck, which has no air-conditioning or open sun deck. There are toilet facilities on board, and tea, coffee, beer, soft drinks, dry sandwiches and other snacks are sold.

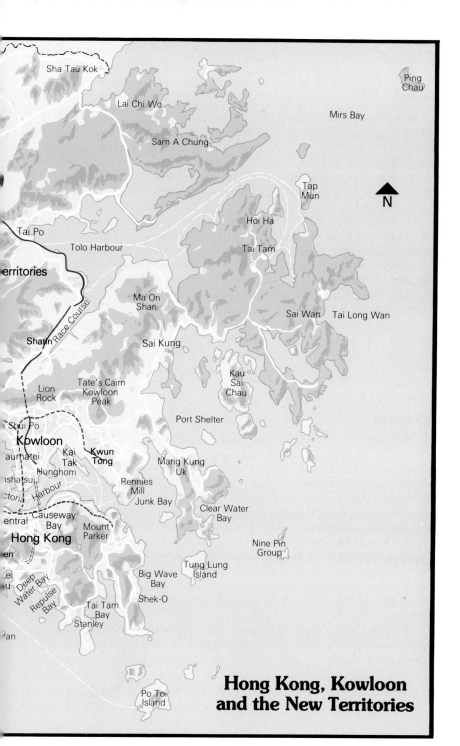

N

Hong Kong, Kowloon and the New Territories

Buses

Hong Kong's heavily used bus network reaches most corners of the colony. Buses are in the hands of three private companies — in Kowloon and the New Territories the Kowloon Motor Bus Company operates more than 200 routes; on Hong Kong Island the China Motor Bus Company has some 100 routes, with additional cross-harbour buses run together with the KMB; and the New Lantau Bus Company runs a much smaller scale bus service on Lantau.

First-time visitors to Hong Kong are likely to have difficulty working out the exact route a bus will take (the terminus is displayed on the front) and locating appropriate bus-stops. Bus routes are constantly changing, and published timetables outdated. The HKTA are experienced at explaining the intricacies of the bus system to visitors, and it does provide an efficient way of getting around, if not always comfortable — a ride on a shabby, unsprung bus during peak hours or on a hot summer's day is not fun.

Fares change according to route length, ranging from 60 cents upwards. Drop the money into a coin box (the amount is usually displayed by the box) as you get on; no change is given. There are no conductors on board, and you should not rely on any help from the driver in recognizing your destination. To signal you want to get off at the next stop, push the black rubber strip on the ceiling.

Minibuses

The cream-coloured minibuses, with a red stripe, that weave in and out of the traffic stopping virtually anywhere, provide a quick, convenient way of getting about once you work out how to use them. These 14-seater privately-owned vehicles run mostly on major routes in direct competition with double-decker buses or trams, and cover the distances considerably faster than their rivals. Apart from certain restricted zones, the mini-bus can stop just about anywhere — hold out your hand to stop the bus, and simply shout at the driver when you want to get out. Choosing the right minibus is sometimes difficult — although the final destination is displayed on the front, the sign is sometimes too small to see until the bus has whizzed past. Fares (shown in the front window and paid when you get off) are a little higher than ordinary buses, and fluctuate with demand, sometimes tripling when it rains.

Minibuses with a green stripe are known as maxicabs and are under tighter government control. They are designed to serve areas which do not have a full bus service. Fares (usually paid when you get in), frequency and stopping places are all fixed.

There are no published lists of minibus routes, but the HKTA has details.

Trains

Hong Kong has only one railway line — a section of the old Canton-Kowloon Railway which first opened in 1911. The line has seen grander days, when it formed the last leg of the London-Hong Kong run terminating in a splendid railway station of European proportions (only the clock tower now stands) on the waterfront.

But the railway is still well used today. Starting from the new Kowloon station at Hunghom (right beside the cross-harbour tunnel) trains take around 33 minutes to reach Sheung Shui, stopping at Mongkok, Shatin, the Chinese University, Tai Po Kau, Tai Po and Fanling on the way — an interesting journey with picturesque views across Tolo harbour and glimpses of New Territories rural life. Unfortunately only those with special permits, or travel documents for China, can go on up to the final stop at the border where Canton-bound passengers climb down and walk across Lowu bridge into China. There are also two through-trains a day from Kowloon to Canton and special trains for Shatin racecourse.

Electrification and modernization of the railway was completed in July 1983 — double-tracked, streamlined high-speed cars with a passenger capacity of 775 each unit are now in operation. Trains run from Kowloon between 6.39am and 11.21pm and from Lowu from 6am to 11.15pm (7.19pm is the last train transit to China). Check with the HKTA or at the , station for up-to-date time table information. Tickets have to be bought at the station just before the train leaves.

Avoid trains during the statutory holiday breaks, such as Chinese New Year and Easter, when thousands of people visit friends and relations in China, or on sunny Sundays when campers, walkers and barbequers swarm to the New Territories. The station can be bedlam on these occasions.

Rickshaws

A rickshaw in the traffic chaos of Central or Tsimshatsui looks as incongruous as it would in New York or London. Nevertheless a few old rickshawmen lurk by the Star Ferry concourses on both sides of the harbour seeking out tourist custom. They will happily pose for pictures and bargain vehemently for a large fee afterwards.

The Peak Tram

Hong Kong's famous funicular railway, the Peak tram, is much more than just the quickest way to get to the top of Hong Kong Island's highest mountain — it is one of the most thrilling ways of seeing Hong Kong.

The tram rises seemingly vertically (the incline is in fact 45°) from the mass of Central's highrise blocks, reaching Victoria Peak a thousand feet higher in around eight minutes. Views are magnificent — across Victoria harbour to Kowloon and the distant hills of China, and down along the northern strip of Hong Kong Island to Wanchai and Causeway Bay.

Designed by a Scot with experience in Scottish Highland railways, and opened in 1888, the Peak tram retains a solid late Victorian aura, with green caste-iron cars, smooth mahogany slatted wooden seats and midway tram stations not unlike miniature versions of British Rail branchline stations. Those apprehensive about the gradient (the steepest in the world it is said), the system's age, or the slight bounce at midway stops, should be comforted by the tram's perfect safety record.

The terminus in Central is a little way up Garden Road, opposite the US Consulate. There is a continuous service from 6am until midnight. Tickets costs $4. The tram is no mere tourist attraction, as the numbers of pinstripped commuters, schoolchildren and wives going shopping in Central affirm, but there are always long queues of sightseers, local as well as foreign, on Sundays.

Trams

Despite perpetual rebuilding of the urban areas, Hong Kong's tram system, which was first set up in 1904, not only miraculously survives, but is actually thriving.

The distinctive old green double-decker trams rattle along the north side of Hong Kong Island from Kennedy Town through Central to Causeway Bay, North Point and Shaukeiwan, with a single branchline to Happy Valley. They are not for anyone in a hurry, but for a visitor with a window seat on top and a breeze to relieve summer heat, this is a pleasant way to look at some of the most lively parts of town. Otherwise trams should be used for short trips only; with their exceptionally low ceilings they have not been designed for the taller western traveller. In rush hour more people pile onto them than would seem humanly possible.

You enter at the back of the tram, making your way forward (no easy task in a crowded tram) paying as you exit at the front. The fare is a flat rate of 60 cents. The final destination of the tram is marked on the front (not all go as far as Shaukeiwan or Kennedy Town). If you are heading to Causeway Bay or further east, make sure you do not get on a tram that will branch off at Happy Valley.

The Mass Transit Railway (MTR)

Hong Kong's latest major engineering triumph, the MTR, has revolutionized transport between Hong Kong Island and Kowloon. The first 9.7 miles of underground line were opened in February 1980, stretching from Kwun Tong in east Kowloon, down Nathan Road and under the harbour to Central. It is the first underground rail system to be totally airconditioned.

The MTR, which boasts the largest stations in the world, can cope with 1.2 million journeys a day. Each of its vast smooth-gliding carriages seat only 48 (on slippery stainless steel seats) but there is room for more than 300 to stand.

Plastic magnetically encoded tickets, credit card size, are bought from machines which give no change, and are then slotted through the entrance turnstile and later devoured by an exit turnstile when the journey is over. Look on the concourse walls for directions to the appropriate exit; stations tend to have several, some of them considerable distances apart.

A 6.5 mile link from Tsuen Wan in West Kowloon was completed in 1984. The Island Line, along Hong Kong Island's northern shore, links Chai Wan and Sheung Wan and comprises 14 stations. The greater part of the line, Chai Wan to Admiralty, was just completed in May 1985, and the remainder from Admiralty to Sheung Wan will be completed sometime in 1986.

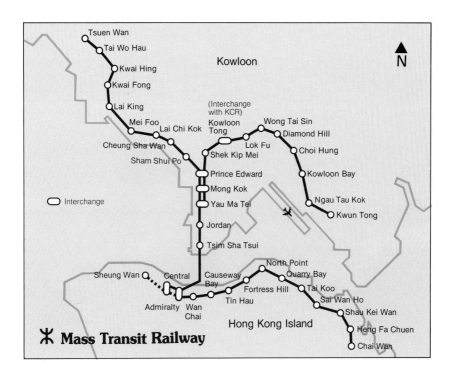

Food in Hong Kong

by Harry Rolnick

With more than 95% of Hong Kong's people originally from the bordering province of Canton, it is hardly surprising that the overwhelming majority of the colony's 8000-odd restaurants should be devoted to Cantonese cuisine. Fortunately, just as France could be called the apex of European cuisine, so Canton has long been regarded as the most subtle, multifarious, ingenious and interesting of all the Chinese cuisines.

Equally fortunately, though, the Cantonese aren't quite so prejudiced against other cuisines as, say, the metropolitan Parisian might be against 'inferior' foreign dishes. The Cantonese may habituate himself to his native fare, but he has nothing against a spicy night out with some Szechuan food, he loves his oily, warming Shanghai dishes during the wintertime, and for those *very* special occasions, he'll impress everybody with a Peking banquet, the centre of which is Peking duck or Hangchow Beggar's Chicken.

The third part of Hong Kong's culinary good fortune is that the expatriates, predominantly from Scotland and England, have eschewed their own provinciality, and are willing to indulge in foods from all over Asia — if only as a reminder that much of these exotic foods came from one-time colonies. In addition the burgeoning tourist trade over the past decade has meant that many European restaurants of high quality have made their mark here, to the benefit of all.

The China Syndrome

For a casual visitor, the words 'Chinese restaurant' might suffice, but to those who truly enjoy their eating, the words mean practically nothing. Outside of the major differences in the regions, there are so many different types of restaurants, so many seasonal imperatives and so many different ways of eating, that the syndrome of Chinese food is virtually infinite.

On the most informal and least expensive scale are the street restaurants or noodle stalls. The best of these are on the side streets of Wanchai and behind the Lee Theatre on Causeway Bay (these are on Hong Kong side), or along Shanghai Street, on Kowloon side. The most popular for tourists are in the 'Poor Man's Nightclub', hundreds of stalls set up adjacent to the Macau Ferry Pier. Naturally there are no written menus. One walks from stall to stall pointing to what looks good, then sits down on a rickety chair by a more rickety table. Everything will be delivered to the table, and somehow the bill will be totted up by the various entepreneurs, usually with faultless accuracy.

The variety can extend from offal of ox, pig and cow to the freshest seafood (the latter surprisingly expensive for such an important fishing town). There are a dozen different kinds of noodles, noodle soup with wonton or meats and vegetables. And of course nearly everything is accompanied by rice. It's usually good fun, if you don't mind being stared at during the meal.

Up a few grades are the morning dim sum restaurants. The best are listed in the Restaurants section (under 'D'). But almost every Cantonese-style restaurant serves *dim sum* from 6am through lunch. *Dim sum* has two distinct advantages. First, as they are usually on display, passed around in little bamboo baskets, one need not understand a word of Cantonese to order. Simply point a finger, and the basket is placed on the table. One need not even worry about a written bill. At the end of the meal, the baskets are added up, and the price is paid, invariably, very reasonable too. The other advantage is that these little Chinese *hors d'oeuvres* — literally 'little hearts' — are delicious.

Fresh seafood

Third up the scale are the ordinary meals in Chinese restaurants. Except for very small restaurants (equivalent to indoor noodle stalls) and the monstrous ones in far-out sections of Hong Kong where foreigners rarely wander, nearly all restaurants have English-language menus. Unfortunately, even with lists of up to 500 different dishes, some of the best aren't even mentioned. Your best bets in this case are a) to enlist a friendly waiter to help you; b) go with some Chinese friends; c) if you spot something good on another table, don't hesitate to ask what it is.

Another point to remember is that Chinese dishes here are very different than those in your own country. The great pride of Cantonese food is that it is always fresh. And as the greens in London or seafood in San Francisco are different from the *choi* or shrimp of Hong Kong, the ingredients and tastes will be unlike those you know.

Most important, though, is how to order. Remember that democracy at a large Chinese party is unheard of. The host (or, if going Dutch treat, the self-appointed leader), will take the menu and decide what others will have. After checking food prejudices (i.e., whether eel or pork or fish lips is acceptable to all), the Leader should begin ordering. A basic plan is to start with a cold dish, then order one beef, one pork, one vegetable, one seafood or fish, one soup, some noodles or fried rice. Traditionally, one should order a single plate for each member of the party, plus one more. The waiter will determine what size platter to bring: for up to four, a small serving will do, up to nine or ten a medium size dish, and after that, a large portion.

As Chinese food has been an 'in' thing in most Occidental capitals, most visitors have some idea of the differences between the regions. But here is a rundown.

Cantonese: The best Cantonese food in the world is in Hong Kong. The preparations are traditional (as they are in Canton itself), but the ingredients come not only from China but Hong Kong (the New Territories was once called 'The Emperor's Rice Bowl' for its richness) and the rest of the world. The emphasis is on fast cooking to bring dishes to the apex of their natural taste and colour. No greasy dishes are ever served. If they aren't fast-fried in a minimum of oil, they are steamed or broiled. Few spices are used but sauces are many. The Guangdong coast supplies remarkable seafood, as well as an abundance of fowl, meat and vegetables, as well as an endless variety of mushrooms. Truly this is the world's greatest cuisine — as even the Parisian practitioners of *nouvelle cuisine* are happy to point out.

Pekingese: The arid desert of northern China has little in the way of natural ingredients, unlike tropical and sub-tropical Canton. But as Peking was since early times the capital of China, the best provender was sent up to the Emperor's palaces, and some fine recipes were devised. Most popular is Peking duck, of course, but the Mongolian hot pot is popular, as are the lamb and mutton dishes, especially during the winter. One rarely eats rice with this food. Instead, ask for some dumplings (perhaps half steamed, half fried), and you should wind up the meal with noodles and vegetables.

Szechuanese: This is the spiciest of all Chinese foods. Garlic, pepper, fennel, coriander and star anise all grow in Szechuan province and are added liberally to the steamed, simmered, smoked dishes. These include excellent seafood, superb fowl and eggplant, as well as an intriguing sour-and-hot soup to finish off the meal. Be prepared for a *lot* of garlic.

Shanghainese: This is a bit greasier than some, a little sweeter, and the dishes are fried for a long time in sesame or soy sauce. The seafood — especially eel and winter crab — is awfully good, and the portions are enormous. The dumplings are very good, and the little shrimp with pieces of garlic and pepper are excellent. Many of the dishes come from other provinces, befitting Shanghai's status as the largest port in China and its most cosmopolitan city.

Hakka and **Chiu Chow**: Both of these cuisines come from the south of China, and neither are very popular outside the Far East. But Chiu Chow food is gutsy, with thick sharksfin soup, goose doused in soy sauce, excellent seafood and all kinds of birds nest dishes. Usually these restaurants don't close down until 3am. Hakka food comes from a nomadic people who must preserve their foods. Consequently, many of the best dishes are salted down (like the salt chicken or salted cabbage), and are not terribly appealing, save that the mixed vegetable dish, *lo han*, is probably the best of all vegetable dishes.

In the top grade of all Chinese food comes the **Man Han Banquet** — and should you be so lucky as to be invited on one of these rare occasions, do go. A traditional banquet isn't simply one dinner: it consists of at least three days of dining. And of the 100-odd dishes, not a single one is duplicated.

To quote from one of the Chinese sages: 'Let there be plenty of food and plenty of clothing, and propriety and righteousness will flourish.'

The Tables of Asia

With immigrants from all parts of Asia, and with a European population always on the lookout for different foods, it is little wonder that Hong Kong can serve dishes from all over the Orient. Granted, some of the restaurants aren't always the cleanest (one thinks immediately of the Indian restaurants in Chungking Mansions, on Kowloon side), but for the most part health laws are so stringent that one can eat in safety.

For the record, countries represented include India (mainly North India, but with a few Madrasi dishes served in Chungking Mansions), Pakistan (virtually the same as North India), Indonesia (spicy, with coconut milk and *sambal* hot sauces), Malaysia (virtually the same as Indonesia, but with less variety, as the restaurants are run by Chinese), Japan, Korea (very spicy, marvellous barbecued beef), Thailand (spicy curries, with a plethora of coriander; fine hot salads, soups filled with tangy lemon grass, and good curries), and Vietnam where the food is mild except for the vinegar and includes dewy-fresh greens, mint, lettuce etc.

Food from the long-nosed barbarians

Traditionally, European food was as much an anathema to the Chinese as were Europeans themselves. In multi-national Hong Kong, this has obviously changed — and rare is the younger Chinese who doesn't indulge almost daily at fast food shops like McDonald's or Dairy Queen.

Every hotel has its restaurants, and first-class hotels nearly always have European managers. Prices are fairly reasonable for cuisine, fairly unreasonable for wines. (Hong Kong is duty-free in everything except cigarettes and liquor and mild, mild women.) The best bargains are the buffets. The Hilton, Furama, Peninsula, and Hongkong hotels all have superb buffets, at prices from $80 to $100.

At private restaurants, the prix fixe lunches are about one-third the price of *à la carte* meals. Gaddi's Chesa and Au Trou Normande are usually expensive, so these set lunches fall into the bargain class.

Outside of the hotels, a number of 'ethnic' restaurants are around: little Mexican cafes, pizzerias, a few delicatessens, some Hungarian food, and around Wanchai, one can have very inexpensive ordinary European dishes.

At first-class restaurants outside the hotels included in the list on Page 122 prices are usually a little less, though wine is still high. And at these places, you can hobnob with residents of Hong Kong, not simply fellow travellers.

The main rule in Hong Kong dining out is never ever to be afraid of trying new dishes and restaurants off the beaten path. If Hong Kong people are handsome, healthy, hard-working and hearty, they are the prime heirs of the dictum offered by Confucius, way back in the Fifth Century B.C. 'Great food,' he said, 'is the first happiness.'

Shopping

It's no exaggeration to say that Hong Kong's tourist industry was built on the attraction of its shopping, which accounts for 60% of all visitors' expenditure, or about $8,220 million in 1984. There are various reasons for Hong Kong's being one huge department store. Almost all goods are imported duty free, which in theory makes them cheaper than anywhere else, including their country of origin. In fact astronomical rents in central shopping districts have forced some prices up to offset this advantage. Many store owners have moved a few blocks from Central and Nathan Road and a wise shopper should follow them.

Fortunately more and more goods are made in Hong Kong and there is a growing market in clothes, electronics, toys and optical equipment designed for export but available in local shops at prices far below the imported equivalents, and there is a healthy domestic market of six million keen consumers.

Hong Kong's skilled, industrious workers have long since left their sweatshops but they are still willing to labour at all hours to sew a suit, carve a camphorwood chest or fashion a piece of jewellery to order. This is the basic reason why Hong Kong is still unrivalled as the place for custom-made items of excellent quality at very reasonable prices.

In recent years, Hong Kong has benefitted from being the prime showcase for goods made in China. Ranging from garments to bicycles, medicine to musical instruments, these products are far more abundant and invariably cheaper than in stores in China itself and many souvenirs from the People's Republic are bought in Hong Kong.

Any shopping expedition in Hong Kong can be daunting. No one has ever counted the number of shops but 1300 of them are members of the Hong Kong Tourist Association. These are to be recommended as the HKTA undertakes to deal with any complaints from customers and stores can be struck off for dishonest dealings. (Watch out for the HKTA junk logo in the window.) The HKTA also helps visitors by listing all their shop members, together with a price guide, in a free booklet **'The official guide to the best of Hong Kong shopping'**, available at any of the association's information offices.

There are three major shopping areas for tourists. Central District, around the super-deluxe arcades of the Landmark building, is the most expensive, but walk a few blocks west and the prices tumble. Tsimshatsui is packed with shops on the Golden Mile of Nathan Road and streets leading from it. Here the competition is very keen and comparison shopping is well worthwhile. Probably the lowest prices are found in Causeway Bay, where most of the customers are local residents.

Dedicated shoppers will enjoy exploring the many small stores in these areas. Others might prefer conveniently compact shopping centres, especially when it's hot or raining. The arcades found in many hotels are the most convenient but remember the rent-price tag connection! For a very wide range of shops and very reasonable prices the best bet is the vast air-conditioned complex of Ocean Terminal and Ocean Centre, adjoining the Hongkong hotel.

In addition there are plenty of department stores. For first class imports visit Lane Crawford or Shui Hing, for Japanese products Daimaru, Sogo, Matsuzakaya, Isetan and Mitsukoshi have branches in Hong Kong and for a wealth of goods made in China go to one of the Yue Hwa stores in Kowloon or China Products in Causeway Bay.

In these stores prices are fixed but in other shops and at street stalls bargaining is expected. In fact customers are regularly offered a 'special price' or a discount of 10% and some persistence will usually result in a further reduction. Be warned however that this only applies when you use cash. Most shops accept the major credit cards but the handling charge cancels out the discount. Also shops will often take foreign currency in payment, but don't expect to get the best exchange rate.

Except for department stores and shops in high class arcades, which open six days a week 10am to 6pm, all shops are open every day 10am to 10pm.

Garments and Fabrics

Every kind of ready-made garment is sold in Hong Kong from Pucci and Pierre Cardin high fashion to Chinese-made padded jackets to overruns of designers jeans (sold for a song at Stanley Market and in Cheung Chau). Furs made from Siberian or Chinese skins are good buys, especially when made to order. Given the skill of local tailors and the availability of reasonably priced fabrics — from Chinese silk brocade to British woollens — Hong Kong is the ideal place to have clothes made to measure. Allow time for two or three fittings or give the tailor a garment to copy. Many satisfied customers continue to order clothes after they return home, usually with excellent results.

Shoes

There are ready-made shoes available in Hong Kong but usually in small sizes. Several stores specialize in custom-made shoes and boots for foreigners, and these are excellent.

Jewellery

Gold is imported duty-free and is relatively cheap. At most jewellery stores the day's price of gold is displayed (so many dollars per *tael*, the equivalent of 1.2 troy ounces) and gold jewellery is as much an investment

as an ornament. All kinds of precious and semi-precious stones
bought, set or unset, and expert craftsmen can follow individual des...
give you a unique ring or necklace. Hong Kong is one of the world's m...
diamond traders and by and large dealers are honest and helpful. If in
doubt call the Diamond Importers Association at 5-235497.

Jade is considered a stone from heaven by the Chinese and a valued
talisman. As a result Hong Kong has the world's best selection of jade but
prices tend to be high. For cheap pieces visit the Jade Market [see
Kowloon], for more expensive jewellery and figurines know what you're
doing.

Many stores sell ivory objects and Hong Kong is one of the biggest
importers of tusks (many smuggled in), but do your bit for conservation and
ignore it.

Wanchai Market

Cameras and Optical Equipment

Hundreds of Hong Kong stores sell the very latest in photographic
equipment and the choice is bewildering. Sales staff are usually well
informed and helpful. Prices tend to be 10% off list and you can ask to see
the list. Hong Kong-produced binoculars are among the best in the world.

Watches and Clocks

Hong Kong is the world's largest manufacturer of watches, mostly of the
cheaper variety but very reliable. For the best prices try the shops along

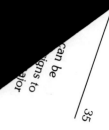

;ide streets of Kowloon and always bargain
ɾand make sure you get the manufacturer's
.redible discounts, there have been cases of
ℓ Rolex or Omega faces.

ıd Equipment

,adin's Cave for stereo enthusiasts and kids of all
ages. ˌˌ   .ll of the remarkable 'toys' of the new electronic age,
from complex   ,ystems to tiny calculators which do everything except
make your morning ɩea, and pocket-sized electronic games. The dealers like
to keep their stock moving so it pays to bargain.

Antiques and Handicrafts

You're not likely to find a Ming vase for $10 but there are still bargains
in Chinese antiques to be uncovered in Hong Kong's Hollywood Road, or
'Cat Street', area (now sadly diminished by redevelopment). There are also
'instant' antiques, faithful reproductions of classic pieces which nevertheless
show the enduring skill of Chinese craftsmen. For absolutely genuine
antiques, at appropriate prices, there is Charlotte Horstmann, and Chinese
Arts & Crafts. The latter stores also sell beautiful handicrafts such as painted
scrolls, lacquered fans, paper cut-outs, embroidered table linen and many
other excellent gifts and souvenirs.

Furniture and Carpets

Chinese craftsmen keep up the tradition of great woodwork in Hong
Kong, and custom-made chests, side-boards, tables and chairs — carved,
inlaid with mother-of-pearl or gilded — are spectacular buys. To
complement the furniture special stores sell Persian, Indian and Chinese
carpets, both antique and modern, as well as locally-made Tai Ping [see
New Territories].

Miscellaneous

Hong Kong has probably the best selection of luggage, brief cases and
other carrying bags anywhere. They range from very inexpensive canvas
suit cases to custom-made bags of the finest leather. For the former try
shopping alleys and the lanes, for the latter visit a leather goods shop.

Hong Kong-made spectacles are excellent and the standard of opticians
very high so it might be worth your while to get your glasses here. Eye tests
are free.

As a final indication of the range of custom-made items available in this
market where all things are possible, you can have a name chop made with
your name in Chinese characters for a few dollars, or you can order a
specially created yacht or pleasure junk for a few hundred thousand.

Arts and Entertainment

Hong Kong has long been thought a cultural void, but today that image is less justified. Although Hong Kong does not compete with neighbouring Tokyo for numbers of distinguished visiting musicians, it does attract its share of worthwhile international soloists, orchestras, small dance companies and chamber ensembles, largely supported by the Urban Council and various cultural organizations. Pop concerts given by international and local stars are put on by commercial concerns usually at the Lee Theatre.

Venues

For the moment Hong Kong's cultural life centres on the **City Hall**, which has a 1500-seat concert hall and small 470-seat theatre (by the Star Ferry Concourse on Hong Kong Island), and the **Arts Centre** (on an unprepossessing section of Wanchai waterfront). In Wanchai the new **Queen Elizabeth Stadium**, opened in 1980, can ostensibly cope with artistic as well as sports events, although visiting ballet and theatre companies, and their audiences, have complained that the stadium, with computerized scoreboards, prominent clocks and steeply raked seats, smacks of sports, not arts. The first of several cultural complexes planned for new towns, the $25 million **Tsuen Wan Town Hall**, can be reached by a hover ferry from Central, although the Hall's policy of only selling tickets at their box office is daunting for those who like to book seats in advance.

The 12,500-seat **Hong Kong Coliseum**, opened in 1983, is one of the largest and best equipped multi-purpose indoor stadiums in Asia. It is fitted with the latest electronic sound and lighting system. The arena can be over-laid with wooden flooring or a rubberised surface to cater for various sports events and can be converted into an ice-skating rink for ice shows or recreational skating. Presentations include performances by top artists, family entertainment shows and sports events.

The Arts Centre is a curiously-angled metallic grey building on the harbour side of Gloucester Road, linked to Wanchai proper by a footbridge. Here, on a diminutive government-granted plot, Hong Kong ingenuity has found a way to provide facilities for all the arts. The Centre (opened in 1977) contains 3 theatres, 2 floors of galleries, and numerous practice and education areas.

The Arts Centre believes in diversity·as the key to a thriving cultural life. There are some thousand presentations a year, three quarters of which are put on by outsiders renting facilities, and a quarter organized by the Centre. The result is a cultural programme which has ranged widely, often incongruously, across the entire spectrum from the London Old Vic

Company's Merchant of Venice to a Cantonese Wizard of Oz, from the Amadeus Quartet to a regular Saturday jazz session, or from Norwegian graphics to paintings by Chinese masters.

The Arts Centre is open to the public seven days a week from 8am till midnight. There are two Young's restaurants — one offers Chinese food in upmarket surroundings, the other, with a bar for drinks before a show, serves European food. Exhibitions and performance times are listed in the Centre's monthly programme, available in the foyer, and the box office is open 10am-8.15pm.

Arts Festivals

There are three annual festivals which may interest visitors. Although the best seats tend to be snapped up weeks in advance by residents, returns may be available just before the performance begins. The **Festival of Asian Arts**, held around October, is a gathering ground for dance, music and visual presentations of varying quality from most countries in the region.

In February, the **Hong Kong Arts Festival** provides the biggest annual importation of western arts. Delighted residents — a hefty proportion of them expatriates — are treated to a month's concentrated diet of imported western concerts, theatre, mime, jazz and dance, with a token Chinese production — nothing too innovative, but all thoroughly pleasant.

Hong Kong's **International Film Festival**, usually held in the spring, is an unstructured feast for residents who are deprived of the best of the world's cinema by Hong Kong's conservative cash-conscious distributors. But, apart from the Asian Cinema section, it is unlikely to be as exciting for visitors from western cinematic centres.

Cinema

International though Hong Kong may be in many respects, its cinematic offerings are disappointingly second-rate. Apart from the lastest Hollywood Award-winning films, little of the best of American or European cinema finds its way onto the commercial circuit. And when it does, it may well be cut, either by the censor or by the theatre manager whose main concern is fitting the film into a neat two-hour programme.

Hong Kong possesses only one commercial cinema that could claim a luxury label: the plush Palace in the World Trade Centre. For the rest, be prepared for noisy comings and goings throughout the film, smokers and small children in the audience, and the possibility of distorted sound. Seats are generally inexpensive, ranging upwards from $10. For films newly released in Hong Kong tickets should be bought in advance from the cinema box office. And double check that you are going to the film you want; box office failures are taken off overnight with no warning.

The showings by two film clubs, Studio One and the Phoenix Cine Club, are unfortunately for members only. For the general public the Goethe Institute and the Alliance Francaise run film programmes (except during the summer months) at various venues. Look out for advertisements at City Hall or telephone the Goethe Institute at 5-270088 and the Alliance Francaise at 5-277825.

Chinese Opera

Enthusiasm for traditional Chinese opera is still very much alive in Hong Kong. There are said to be some 500 full-time professional actors involved in this spectacular (and bewildering to the uninitiated) form of theatre.

The best opera is given by the companies from China that visit Hong Kong occasionally. Little information on these superb troupes penetrates through to the English language press (keep an eye out for a single advertisement or news item). Performances, usually at the Sunbeam Theatre in North Point or at the Lee Theatre in Causeway Bay, are always sold out, the percentage of non-Chinese in the audience negligible. Otherwise, there may be an opera put on by the Urban Council at City Hall or in public parks, or poor quality performances nightly at Lai Chi Kok Amusement Park, or the operas mounted by street or temple organizations to coincide with religious festivals. The HKTA may be able to direct you to some of these performances.

Most of the opera in Hong Kong is Cantonese, a glittery offshoot of more classical Peking Opera. Costumes are more garish, sets more elaborate, and traditional instruments are supplemented by western ones, sometimes even an electric guitar. The high-pitched falsetto of Peking Opera is replaced by lower voices singing in the Cantonese dialect. Other regional forms of opera presented include Chiu Chow, Fukien Stilt Opera, and occasionally Yueh Opera (all female performers) for the Shanghainese community, and classical Peking Opera.

The Media

Radio and Television Recent figures indicate that 98% of the colony's households have a television. There are four channels, two in English, two in Chinese, which put out mostly mediocre television with the high spots often far into the night. For English language radio programmes, government-financed RTHK put out Radio 3 (news, light music), Radio 4 (news, current affairs, classical music, some BBC programmes) and Radio 5 (BBC World Service). There is also one English language commercial station and one run by the British Forces Broadcasting Service.

Press The people of Hong Kong are enthusiastic newspaper readers. Of the 72 newspapers published, only a handful are in English, the major ones being the *South China Morning Post*, the *Asian Wall Street Journal* and the *Hongkong Standard*. Amongst weeklies, the *Far Eastern Economic Review* is outstanding, giving the most authoritative coverage of the Asian region.

Finding out What's On in Hong Kong

Unfortunately Hong Kong has no single comprehensive guide to what's on, and visitors, like residents, have to search through several different sources. Some of the following may be useful:

The South China Morning Post A selection of films at commercial cinemas are listed in the classified section. A daily 'Events and Reminders' list and a 'Keeping in Touch' section (with comment and brief news items) cover some current arts events, but neither are comprehensive. Sports coverage is good. Advertisements for presentations with commercial backing often appear singly elsewhere in the paper. Daily, $2.00

The Hong Kong Standard Advertisements for the commercial cinema appear on the arts page. There is full sports coverage. Daily, $1.50

TV and Entertainment Times An 'Out and About' column details a range of events for the week — an incongruous mix of amateur theatricals, cooking classes, exhibitions, major imported arts. Weekly from Wednesday, $5

City News A monthly newspaper containing a full list of performances at the City Hall, sports events organized or sponsored by the Urban Council, and a programme of entertainments on at the Queen Elizabeth Stadium. Free, available in the City Hall.

Arts Centre programme for the month: A leaflet listing all presentations at the Arts Centre. Free, available at the Arts Centre.

Queen Elizabeth Stadium programme for the month: A leaflet listing all sports events, performances and classes taking place at the stadium. Free, available at the stadium box office.

Orient A weekly newspaper produced by the HKTA. Its 'This Week' column is reasonably comprehensive and one of the few sources for news of Chinese opera performances. Free, at hotels, HKTA offices.

Television and radio: On television there are five-minute programmes. 'What's On' on Radio 3 at 8.30am is the most comprehensive. ATV and TVB, the two English-language television stations, broadcast similar information, but with changing schedules. Check the newspaper for exact timings.

Box Offices:

City Hall 5-229928 and 5-229511	Open daily 11am-9.30pm
Arts Centre 5-280626	Open daily 10am-8.15pm
Queen Elizabeth Stadium 5-756793	Opening hours vary with events
Tsuen Wan Town Hall 0-440144	Open 12.30-9.30pm

Nightlife

Some people say that Hong Kong's nightlife died with the end of the American involvement in the Vietnam War — US servicemen spent their rest and recreation here — while others claim it never existed in the exotic and erotic style of Bangkok and Manila.

No-one doubts that Hong Kong's night centres have lost some of the atmosphere of the '50s and '60s. There are fewer US Shore Patrol officers nowadays, and most of the night-clubs are restrained compared with their counterparts in Thailand and the Philippines. Nonetheless, Hong Kong does offer a large number of bars, nightclubs, discos, massage parlours and escort services which range from the sophisticated and ludicrously overpriced to the extremely sordid, with enough choice to satisfy an equally wide range of tastes.

The two areas for night entertainment best known to visitors are Wanchai and Causeway Bay on Hong Kong Island, and Tsimshatsui in Kowloon. Most of Wanchai's activities centre on the bustling grid of crowded streets of which Lockhart Road is the main thoroughfare. The small tailors and tattooists, the pavement workshops, the cooking smells at the many food stalls, and the glow of neon lights still give Wanchai a special atmosphere. This was the world of Richard Mason's Suzie Wong, and the thoroughly respectable Luk Kwok Hotel is said — but not by the management — to be one of the locations where William Holden and Nancy Kwan shot the film. Across the harbour, Hankow Road and Nathan Road which flank the Peninsula Hotel lead northwards with numerous side streets and alleys where nightclubs and bars are jammed into basements or perched on top of buildings.

Hong Kong's nightlife is enhanced by its names — Red Lips Bar, Pussycat Bar, Pink Lady Night Club, San Francisco Topless, and, inevitably, Suzie Wong Bar. Not unexpectedly the advertised names do not always accurately indicate the activity inside. The terms nightclub, bar, discotheque are used indiscriminately and more often than not mean simply a place where there is music, taped or live, where you can drink, perhaps dance, and where there are quite possibly topless waitresses and more probably bar girls whose main job is to keep the customers drinking.

There are of course plenty of bars where a cocktail can be mixed and drunk uninterrupted in relaxed surroundings. Some hotels have bars where a sophisticated drink can be accompanied by spectacular views. The **Sky Lounge** on the 18th floor of the Sheraton Hotel, Salisbury Road, Tsimshatsui, is one of these, reached by a glass elevator on the outside of the building. For the best close-up views of the busy harbour it would be difficult to match the **Regent Hotel's lobby bar**, opposite the Sheraton, where a vast floor-to-ceiling window gives a magnificent 180° view of Hong Kong Island's waterfront. On the other side of the harbour, the **La Ronda**

bar on the top floor of the Furama Hotel (which does not revolve with the restaurant) gives an equally fine view of the harbour and Kowloon.

Moving downmarket, there are several pleasant bars imbued, to some degree, with a traditional British pub atmosphere. There are no bar girls, but instead, wooden beams, dart boards, brass and leather, a basic menu, and draught British beer. The large **Bull and Bear**, on the ground floor of Hutchinson House in Central, is always crowded, being one of the few pub-bars in the business centre of Hong Kong. The **Old China Hand**, 104 Lockhart Road, Wanchai, is one of the smallest and cosiest. In the basement of the Excelsior Hotel in Causeway Bay, the **Dickens Bar** is slick and noisy — especially when live jazz (on Sundays) or Filipino pop begins in the early evening.

On Kowloon side, the **White Stag**, 72 Canton Road, Tsimshatsui, with a copper topped bar, and wooden beams could be anybody's local country pub — even the menu is traditional. The **Blacksmiths Arms**, 16 Minden Avenue, Tsimshatsui, is more of an urban local, and dishes up large servings of food. Most of these bars open around 11am or noon and serve till around 1am or 2am with a Happy Hour (cheaper prices) normally sometime between 5pm to 7pm.

Hong Kong's Folies Bergere-style show with elaborate choreography for dancers in dazzling costumes has moved to Macau. But one-off shows featuring well-known entertainers are staged several times a year in the **Pink Giraffe** in the Sheraton Hotel. The **Hilton** produces a 'dinner-theatre' two or three times a year and flies in a cast from a popular London West End production. Some of the enormous Chinese restaurants provide a traditional Chinese-flavour floor show, with a meal. These are misleadingly advertised as nightclubs but they provide one of the easiest ways to come into contact with the Cantonese taste in entertainment. At a more casual level, the **Godown** in the basement of Sutherland House, Chater Road, Central, has an unashamedly boisterous bistro atmosphere with live jazz and dancing. On Kowloon side **Ned Kelly's Last Stand**, 11A Ashley Road, Tsimshatsui, adds a rowdy Australian atmosphere to the bistro scene — beer drinking with few frills, live jazz and a menu with interesting-sounding Australian dishes.

Wanchai and Tsimshatsui offer numerous examples of the particularly Asian phenomenon of the hostess club and the rather less elegant girlie bar. They attract tourists and local residents alike, Japanese tourists taking the place of the war-weary American serviceman.

As its name implies the hostess club is strictly for male visitors who require company for an hour or two in a cosy atmosphere with music and a dance-floor, and are willing to pay for it in slots of fifteen minutes or so, tho' the western visitor may be disconcerted by dancing with a partner who is filling in her time sheet at the same time. The **Dai-ichi Club**, 1st floor,

Harbour View Mansion, 257 Gloucester Road, Causeway Bay, is one of the most luxurious and expensive clubs of this kind. The **Kokusai**, 81 Nathan Road, Tsimshatsui, is one of the oldest Japanese-style hostess clubs, and the **Korean Garden**, 119-121 Connaught Road, Central, is naturally enough Korean in atmosphere and style.

Floating Restaurant, Aberdeen

The topless and girlie bars are more difficult to classify — they can change personality overnight. Generally the company of the girls inside is not paid for, but her drinks are. As with the hostess clubs, the girls are available as escorts outside the establishment but in this case a fee is paid to the bar and an extra fee is negotiated with the escort herself.

One of the best-known and reliable bars in Hong Kong is **Bottoms Up** in the basement of 14-16 Hankow Road, Tsimshatsui. This bar has recently celebrated its 14th anniversary and is a favourite with the locally known and internationally famous — possibly because as the general manager says 'we don't hussle our customers — we pamper them'. Topless barmaids serve drinks in three circular bars, but the drinks are delivered by (fully clothed) waiters.

The **Highway**, 53 Lockhart Road, Wanchai, and its sister bar the **Subway**, in the same building, are two of the friendliest topless bars in Wanchai, with Asian waitresses in the upper Highway bar and European or Australian in the basement Subway bar.

Disco fever has waned in Hong Kong and many fast-buck discos which sprang up in the wake of *Saturday Night Fever* have closed. **Disco Disco** is one of the longest running at 40 D'Aguilar Street, Central and currently has a 'Ladies' Night Out' session on Thursdays. Although constantly battling to retain a liquor license, the atmosphere is lively, and the music of a high standard. In a class by itself is the **Manhattan**, the plushest and most expensive of Hong Kong discos. This is the place to look at the smart Chinese disco set relaxing in a circa '30s decor, sunk in satin cushions against a 60-foot photomural of the Manhattan skyline. The disco/cafe cost almost $6 million to deck out and boasts one of the most unusual elevators in Hong Kong.

Poor Man's Nightclub

The cheapest form of night entertainment traditionally presented to tourists are the night markets. Best known is the so-called **Poor Man's Nightclub**, which is set up each evening next to the Rumsey Street Car park near Macau Ferry Pier, and dismantled again around 11pm.

Despite its name, this nightclub is simply a lively market selling cheap clothes and tourist trinkets, with a token fortune in the midst. Most locals head for the seafood in the market's stalls — clams, prawns, mussels, tiger snails. You make your choice, then watch as the food is plunged into bubbling cauldrons of water. The seafood is undoubtedly fresh and appetizing — the surroundings where you eat it, less so.

Museums

Unlike other major cities Hong Kong does not have a large museum. Instead there are four small museums of art, a museum of history, a space museum and a wax museum, all well worth visiting.

Space Museum

Of the four museums centrally located, the Space Museum — on the Kowloon waterfront opposite the Peninsula Hotel — is the most spectacular museum and yet the hardest to visit because the schedule of English-commentary films is often changed. The exhibition halls are open from 2-10pm Mon.-Sat., 10.30am-10pm Sunday and public holidays, closed on Tuesday. Tickets are available only at the museum, for an all-in price of $15.

Opened in October 1980, this $60-million project consists of a 300-seat Space Theatre, a Hall of Solar Sciences, an Exhibition Hall and also a lecture hall, astronomy bookshop and snack bar.

Whatever the **Space Theatre's** programme (changed roughly every six months) you can be sure it will be both beautiful and dramatic. The film is projected onto the 75 feet domed roof. In the centre of the auditorium a weird looking space monster — in fact the Zeiss Planetarium projector — moves up and down on its axis throughout the hour-long show; in addition there is an Omnimax projector with over a 100 precision lenses capable of slotting onto a gigantic 'fish eye', many special effects projectors, and a multi-channel sound system — all automatically controlled by a computer in the centre of the theatre. The result is both absorbing and spectacular. To gain full enjoyment (and to avoid a stiff neck), try and sit as near to the central computer console as possible, as the whole screen is used throughout the show.

The sun is of course the theme of the **Hall of Solar Sciences**. A solar telescope gives the visitor a close look at the anatomy of the star on which we all depend. Other exhibits delve into subjects such as solar phenomena and solar energy with copious use of audiovisual devices and microcomputers; and before you leave there is a quizzing computer to test the knowledge acquired during your visit to the Hall. The **Exhibition Hall** deals with man's advancement in the fields of astronomy and space exploration. One of the most interesting exhibits is the Aurora 7 space capsule in which Scott Carpenter made three orbits of the earth in 1962. It is advisable to make your reservations for all three halls in advance: ring 3-7212361 for current programme times.

The Museum of History is now in two pre-war buildings in Kowloon Park, a little way up Nathan Road, past the Hyatt Hotel. Exhibits chart Hong Kong's archaeological and ethnological background and development. A highlight of the permanent exhibition is the series of detailed models of fishing junks and their tackle, illustrating traditional fishing methods. Special exhibitions, such as 'Hong Kong Before 1841', are invariably fascinating, clearly captioned and well laid out. Those especially interested in 19th and 20th century Hong Kong should ask to see the museum's albums of old photographs. These provide a revealing insight into the colony's development and social life.

Young's Wax Museum

Kowloon's third easily accessible museum is Young's Wax Museum in Basement Two of Miramar Hotel on Nathan Road. Having bought your $5 ticket — not from the lifelike wax vendor — you emerge into a room filled with 21 realistic tableaux. Apart from Marco Polo all are Chinese personalities. The wax models, cast in Hong Kong, are of a high standard. Diligent attention to detail has been paid in the contemporary clothes and furnishings used; the lighting is good and the captions informative. Perhaps the most evocative tableau, set at the end of a passage, is of an early 20th-century soothsayer and her client with the soothsayer's bird pecking at the fortune card of the anxious client. Opening times are from 11am -7pm daily.

Hong Kong Museum of Art

On Hong Kong Island beside the Star Ferry is the Hong Kong Museum of Art on the 10th and 11th floors of the City Hall High Block. On the 10th floor a selection from the museum's Chinese art and antiquities collection is normally on show, while on the 11th floor there are special exhibitions. These cover a broad spectrum of contemporary and period Chinese and western art and photography.

This museum is sadly hampered by its lack of space — its antique picture collection alone consists of over 1000 items. Attractive postcards and various interesting publications are on sale. Opening times are 10am-6pm on weekdays (but closed Thursdays) and Sundays 1pm-6pm.

Fung Ping Shan Museum

Further afield in Pokfulam at the Hong Kong University is the Fung Ping Shan Museum. This imposing building, with its circular main exhibition hall, was originally opened as a museum in 1953 — with the primary purpose of teaching the University's art courses. The museum now possesses a fine bronze collection. Its earliest pieces are ritualistic vessels from the Shang (1600-1027BC) to Zhou (1027-256 BC) Dynasties. Then there are bronze

mirrors from the Han (206 BC-220 AD) to Tang (618-907AD) Dynasties. These strange, predominantly circular objects look more like dolls' shields than mirrors: what could be seen reflected in them is a mystery. From the Yuan Dynasty (1279-1368) there are no fewer than 967 Nestorian Crosses, each of a different design. The Nestorian creed is thought to have reached China in the Tang Dynasty, well before Marco Polo's arrival there. It managed to survive the intervening centuries (with a few hiccups) to regain favour under Khublai Khan who created a Nestorian archbishopric in Peking in 1275. The museum also boasts a fine ceramic collection and late Ming and Ching paintings. Opening times 9.30am-6pm daily. Closed on Sundays and public holidays.

Art Gallery at the Chinese University

The Art Gallery at the Chinese University, Shatin, is predominantly for the purpose of teaching. The museum is in the middle of the impressive University campus. One enters through a modern reproduction of a Chinese courtyard garden. Inside, the exhibition space is divided into four split levels. The museum has several important collections of which the most notable are the Jen Yu-Wen collection, consisting of 1300 items from the Ming Dynasty to recent times, and the Min Chui Society of Hong Kong's bequest of 463 exquisite Ming jade flowers. Opening times 9.30am-4.30pm daily and Sundays 12.30pm-4.30pm.

Lei Cheng Uk

The Lei Cheng Uk Branch Museum (part of the Museum of History) houses a well-preserved tomb of the Eastern Han Dynasty (25-220AD). Following the devastating squatter hut fires of 1954, the tomb was discovered during the foundation work for Shek Kip Mei, Hong Kong's first public housing estate. Subsequent excavation was carried out by the Hong Kong University and the find was opened to the public in 1957. Driving through this densely populated concrete jungle one suddenly comes upon an incongruous grassy knoll beside a park. In front of the tomb stands a small museum building which exhibits drawings and rubbings of life in Han times, as well as actual rubbings from the tomb's patterned bricks and photographs recording the excavation of the site. Replicas of one's worldly possessions to help in the after-life have always played a part in Chinese burial custom and also on display is a selection of the bronze and pottery items found in the tomb — charming model houses complete with animal yards, and pottery storage jars, just like those found today in many a western rustic kitchen. Opening times 10am-1pm and 2-6pm daily (closed Thursdays) and Sundays 1pm-6pm.

Flagstaff House Museum of Tea Ware

The Flagstaff House Museum of Tea Ware is housed in the oldest western style building still existing in Hong Kong today on Cotton Tree Drive. The style of this building demonstrates the architectural characteristics of mid-19th century Hong Kong.

Collection includes about 500 pieces of tea ware mainly of Chinese origin dating from the Warring States Period up to the present day, among which Yixing teapots are the most notable. Opening hours: 10am-5pm except Wednesday.

Festivals

Fu Hsi, a 6th-century scholar, was renowned for wearing a Taoist cap, a Buddhist Scarf and Confucian shoes. This pragmatic approach goes some way towards explaining the religious potpourri that confronts the visitor to Hong Kong. Of its 600 temples, 300 are Buddhist, 200 Taoist, and 100 an amalgam of the two religions. In addition there are 600 Christian establishments. In the Taoist temple you are quite likely to find Buddhist statues and vice versa. Historically the Chinese have found little merit in jealously adhering to one creed but seem to prefer the benefits from several. Thus Hong Kong functions on both the Lunar and western calendars celebrating the religious festivals of both.

Joss spirals in Cheung Chau temple

The **Lunar New Year** — or Chinese New Year — which falls in late January or early February is the most widely observed festival. Each year is assigned to one of 12 animals (which follow each other in rotation), each possessing different characteristics: the legend concerning this 12-year cycle tells how the Lord Buddha summoned to him all earth's animals but only 12 obeyed and, as a reward for their loyalty, he named a year after each one. Your fate in any one year may be determined by the relationship between the animal of the year in question and that of the year of your birth. The coming of a New Year means a period of goodwill, the settling of debts and quarrels and a visit to the fortune-teller. Ancestors are worshipped — the spirit of an uncared for ancestor can turn very nasty — and special attention is paid to the Kitchen God, for it is thought that at the end of each year he returns to the Jade Emperor to report on the family's conduct during the past year. Special food is prepared, often vegetarian, and presents of New Year biscuits (Chau-mai-beng, stamped with messages such as 'Harmony and Property', 'May sons and wealth be yours') are exchanged. To the delight of children they are given little red *lai-si* packets of money — the colour red being lucky. Everywhere you will hear or see the words *Kung hei fat choi* (Best wishes and prosperity) though to young couples the greeting is *Kung hei tim ding* (Best wishes and have more sons).

However for the visitor this thoroughly family festival can be a bleak time. The statutory holiday spans three days but many shops and restaurants close at 10. Thousands of people return to China to visit relatives — so it is also not the best time for a quick trip across the border. Central District, though dressed in decorative lights with the animal of the year shining down from prominent buildings, tends to be deserted. To get an authentic feeling of this family festival, visit one of the flower markets. Narcissi, huge blossom-covered peach branches and mini orange trees are given as symbols of long life and prosperity. The oranges are later dried and stewed to make medicine. The largest market is in Victoria Park, Causeway Bay, where, especially at night, there are row upon row of exquisite blooms, food stalls, side shows and thousands of jostling men, women and children in holiday mood. The end of Chinese New Year on the 15th day is marked by the lighting of traditional lanterns.

The **Springtime Birthday of Tin Hau**, the (Taoist) Empress of Heaven, is lavishly celebrated. To the beat of drums and decked in gay flags and silken banners, laden junks, some carrying lion dancers, sail in convoy to the various temples dedicated to Tin Hau. Nearly all of these are in fishing villages, the most popular being in Joss House Bay. This particular temple was built in 1266 (near the site of an earlier pagoda) and was visited soon after by the last Sung emperor who temporarily established a court in Kowloon. At festival time hundreds of craft moor here, take ashore their offerings and their Tin Hau boat shrines to be blessed for another year by the Taoist priest. It is estimated that 20,000 people visit this temple during the birthday celebrations. Of Tin Hau's earthly existence there are many legends. The daughter of a 10th-century Fukien fisherman, she is reputed to have sailed on a straw mat into the eye of a typhoon and guided an entire fishing fleet to safety. Faith in her supernatural powers continued to grow after her death until, in the Ching Dynasty (1644-1911), she was given the title Empress of Heaven.

In May the three-day **Cheung Chau Bun Festival** is celebrated. Three vast wooden towers, each covered with some 5000 white buns, stamped with a goodwill message, are erected near Pak Tai Temple. The purpose of these bun towers is to appease the hungry spirits of pirate victims, whose mutilated bodies were found in the 1880s on Cheung Chau — a small island on the west side of Hong Kong's archipelago. This Taoist festival is also to give thanks to Pak Tai, Emperor of the North and God of the Sea, for protecting the islanders since the 1770s from various plagues. The festivities include Chiu Chow opera [see Arts and Entertainment], lion dances, stilt dances and a parade of religious tableaux. During this time no meat is eaten. At midnight on the third day a gong sounds and the destruction of the 60-foot bun towers begins. In the past young men scaled them with the object of collecting as many buns as possible; the higher the bun the greater the luck it was supposed to bring them. Since a tower accidentally collapsed, the scramble has been discontinued and the buns are distributed by the priests.

The **Dragon Boat Festival** (Tuen Ng) in June is equally decorative and rather more accessible as the races are held throughout the territory. The story behind these races is a sad one. Chu Yuan, a fourth-century scholar, was so distressed by the corruption of local government officials that he threw himself into the Mei Lo River in Hunan. To scare away marauding fish the local people scattered the water with rice dumplings and beat drums, perhaps rather as one sees Chinese fishermen today, rowing from one end of their net to another, beating a drum, or thrashing the water with a long stick, to scare the fish into their nets. Today the craft used for the races which celebrate this distant event are long, slim and gaily painted, with the ornately carved head and tail of fearsome dragons. Depending on their size, they carry 10 or 20 oarsmen with an additional person beating time on a traditional drum. The races are hotly contested and have even given rise to an international competition, held in Hong Kong a week or so after the festival.

A far more peaceful affair is the **Mid Autumn Festival**. Traditionally this was a harvest festival, but it also had a political significance. During an uprising against the ruling Mongol Yuan Dynasty in the 14th century messages were passed to conspirators in 'moon cakes'. Today these sweet cakes have centres of lotus seeds or duck egg. Several weeks before the

festival one sees charming lanterns — some of traditional shapes, others modern — for sale in all the markets. On the night of the festival it was customary to take the family moon cakes and lanterns to one of the territory's peaks and enjoy the festival by moonlight. However, in recent years a lantern carnival has been organized in Victoria Park, Causeway Bay, so families can now enjoy the peace of a lantern-lit picnic under the trees and (less peaceful) opera and other entertainments at the far end of the park. To see the candle-lit lanterns flickering in the trees is enthralling and well worth a visit.

In contrast there are several festivals throughout the Lunar Calendar less likely to catch the interest of imagination of the tourist: for instance **Ching Ming** and **Chung Yeung** when families simply visit the graves of their ancestors, to clean them and make offerings, or **Yue Lan** (Festival of Hungry Ghosts) when food and paper money is offered to appease the spirits of the dead.

Yachting in Victoria Harbour

Sport

Given the shortage of land in Hong Kong its citizens are surprisingly well provided with sporting facilities. The government has wisely recognized that the availability of a wide range of sports relieves many of the tensions inherent in Hong Kong's cramped living conditions. Practically every sport (including dry skiing and canoe polo) is catered for with emphasis on water-related activities. The opening of the Queen Elizabeth Stadium in Happy Valley, the Victoria Park exhibition tennis courts, and the Hong Kong Coliseum (this $115 million project built over the railway terminus seats 12,500 spectators under cover) make it possible for Hong Kong to stage international sporting events.

However, the most popular sport of all in Hong Kong is horse racing. This is explained by the Chinese love of gambling rather than a love of the horse. Although Hong Kong's Jockey Club was founded in 1884 professional racing was only introduced a decade ago. In the 1984-85 season the total amount wagered was US$2.5 billion which equates to an average per race of an incredible US$3.7 million. (The average in racing mad Britain was a mere US$960,000 in 1980). The Jockey Club administers Hong Kong's racing and holds the government betting monopoly (Hong Kong's only legal form of gambling unless one counts the stock market).

Try and pay a visit to one of the Royal Hong Kong Jockey Club's two courses (at Happy Valley and Shatin, particularly the latter which was completed in 1978 and is equipped with every conceivable modern device). The stands are packed (average attendance per meeting is 34,600), people sit poring over their newspapers, or listening to the latest totaliser odds on their ear hugging transistors. At Shatin there is a vast trackside video matrix — the biggest in the world — on which racegoers in the stands can read the rapidly changing odds, or watch a close-up of the action. It also provides slow motion film and instant replay of a race, and displays information in English and Chinese (the messages being illustrated by animated cartoons). Few racegoers ever venture down to see the actual horses in the paddock. Because of the money involved the air crackles with tension at the start of each race, building up to a crescendo roar from the anxious crowd. The racing season runs from September to May and those interested can buy a guest badge from off course betting offices of the Jockey Club.

Every year the Jockey Club donates a sizeable proportion of its huge surplus to charity and other sports-related facilities such as the Queen Elizabeth Stadium and the Jubilee Sport Centre alongside their racetrack in Shatin. The latter is a $150 million project which provides everything a budding athlete could desire. It is designed to coach Hong Kong's international athletes of the future in those sports in which Hong Kong can excel.

Figure conscious visitors are now able to jog along the Jubilee Sport Centre's 'trim trail' from 7am to 7pm. There are also several gyms (including Hatch and Turk, Nautilus Heath Centre), dance and exercise classes (Arts Centre) readily available in the Central District and Kowloon. At the YMCA there are classes in yoga, judo, *tai chi chuan* and martial arts. For visiting

golfers, the Royal Hong Kong Golf Club has three 18-hole courses at
Fanling in the New Territories and 9 holes at Deepwater Bay (on Hong
Kong Island) but they are available on weekdays only. The Clearwater Bay
Golf and Country Club (in Saikung, tour by HKTA on weekdays) and the
Discovery Bay Golf Club (on Lantau Island 8am-8pm daily) each has a
18-hole course, plus other recreational facilities such as tennis courts,
swimming pool, etc. The tennis enthusiast can use any of the public courts,
it you can get one. You can only book a day in advance (by going in

Racing at Shatin

person, with your passport). These have no equipment for hire but the
Excelsior Hotel Sports Deck with both tennis courts and golf range,
however, does.

For water sports such as water skiing and wind surfing ring the HKTA
who will provide names and numbers to contact. For underwater sports
contact either the Hong Kong Underwater Federation or the YMCA Scuba
Club. However, probably the most enjoyable sport of all for the visitor is
walking — exploring the unknown countryside, enjoying its staggering
views and beautiful flora and fauna and getting the feel of local life from the
villages one passes through. Excellent booklets on the Nature Trails and
Hong Kong's wild life are available from the Government Publication Centre

(behind the Connaught Centre). As well as all important maps, the HKTA produces a series on both urban and rural walks. Also recommended is the book *Selected Walks in Hong Kong* available at most bookshops.

Beaches

It comes as a surprise to some visitors to discover that Hong Kong's rocky coastline is dotted with beaches. Some 38 of these, on the mainland and some islands, are maintained for public use — they are manned during the summer season by life guards and beach cleaners, and offer changing rooms, tents, barbeque pits, refreshments stalls and bathing rafts. The HKTA has a useful small leaflet which locates all maintained beaches, lists the facilities and describes how to get there.

But however enthusiastic the HKTA may be, no realist would deny that the colony's crowded beaches come a poor second to the glorious stretches of sand in nearby Malaysia, Thailand or the Philippines. There may of course be days when beach conditions in Hong Kong are near perfect. The sand may at times be clean (although it is never golden), the water may be as clear as the South China Sea ever is, and midweek the beach may be almost deserted. But the chances of this magic combination are small. Winds and tides carry piles of debris (driftwood, plastic bags and far worse) onto all beaches at some time or other. Heavy rain leaves both sand and sea muddy and grey. On Saturday afternoons, Sundays and public holidays, huge crowds of garrulous swimmers with barbeques and radios descend on beaches almost everywhere in the colony.

The best beaches in Hong Kong are inevitably the most inaccessible. If you have the time (and the weather) to devote a whole day to the beach, then it is possible to treat yourself to an interesting expedition that will give a glimpse of some of the most beautiful parts of Hong Kong. On Lantau the near 3000-feet Lantau and Sunset Peaks form a stunning backdrop to a string of long sandy beaches that stretches along the island's southern shores. On the mainland the beaches of Clearwater Bay in the Sai Kung peninsula are mostly unspoilt, sometimes breathtakingly beautiful. The inaccessibility rule even applies to Hong Kong Island, where the least crowded beach is at Big Wave Bay.

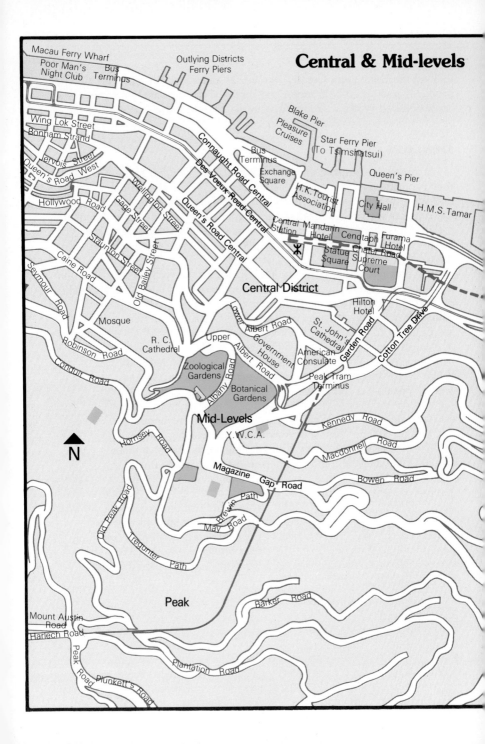

Central & Mid-levels

Macau Ferry Wharf
Poor Man's Night Club
Bus Terminus
Outlying Districts Ferry Piers

Wing Lok Street
Bonham Strand
Jervois Street
Queen's Road West
Hollywood Road
Connaught Road Central
Des Voeux Road Central
Queen's Road Central
Wellington Street
Gage Street
Staunton Street
Old Bailey Street
Caine Road
Seymour Road
Robinson Road
Conduit Road

Bus Terminus
Exchange Square
H.K. Tourist Association

Blake Pier
Pleasure Cruises
Star Ferry Pier (To Tsimshatsui)
Queen's Pier
City Hall
H.M.S. Tamar

Central Mandarin Station Hotel
Cenotaph
Chater Road
Furama Hotel
Statue Square
Supreme Court

Central District

Mosque
R. C. Cathedral
Upper Albert Road
Lower Albert Road
Government House
St. John's Cathedral
American Consulate
Hilton Hotel
Garden Road
Cotton Tree Drive

Zoological Gardens
Albany Road
Botanical Gardens
Peak Tram Terminus

Mid-Levels
Y.W.C.A.

Kennedy Road
Macdonnell Road
Bowen Road

Hornsey Road
Magazine Gap Road

Old Peak Road
Brewin Path
May Road
Tregunter Path

Peak
Barker Road

Mount Austin Road
Harlech Road
Peak Road
Plantation Road
Plunkett's Road

N

Hong Kong Island

The brief history of Hong Kong Island is a story of phenomenal growth. When Britain first occupied it in 1841 it was, in Lord Palmerston's much quoted description 'a barren island with hardly a house upon it'. Today the island is the centre of one of the most buoyant economies in Asia, with some of the highest population densities to be found anywhere.

Hong Kong Island's rapid expansion has consistently astonished the world. The British had been in occupation less than three years when the first governor, Sir Henry Pottinger, reported to England that the settlement had made 'extraordinary and unparalleled progress'. By 1846 the population had doubled (to 24,000 of which 600 were Europeans) and a colonial life style had evolved: horse-racing had started in Happy Valley, amateur dramatics were underway and the Hong Kong Club was founded. Central was the first area to be developed, with insanitary over-crowded Chinese settlements to the east and west of it. Despite continuing bouts of plague and cholera, by the 1870's, sinologist The Reverend James Legge spoke of the northern shore's imposing terraces and magnificent residences, and congratulated the colony on its triumph over difficulties of natural position. Travellers marvelled at the 'Englishness' of the houses and gardens while a guide book extolled the island's magnificent public buildings and hotels. By the turn of the century the population of 300,000 had spread haphazardly from Western to Shaukeiwan and crept up to Midlevels and the Peak. Controlled urban planning and legislation it seemed, even in these early days, never quite kept up with the developers.

With the leasing of the New Territories in 1898, renewed confidence in the colony meant the injection of more public money into constructing reservoirs and reclaiming more land. The south side became more accessible when work on the first road to encircle the whole island began in 1915.

The rocky scrub-covered mountainous terrain, reminding many a British expatriate of Scotland's rugged west coast, looks wholly unsuited to accommodating persistent waves of immigrants. Yet today the 29 square mile island has a population of 1.5 million. Most building has been constricted to the flat, narrow strip along the northern shore, and to small areas around Aberdeen, Repulse Bay and Stanley, spreading with extreme difficulty up steep slopes into chiselled-out terraces, or out into the sea on reclaimed land. To the unaccustomed eye, it seems that every possible building site has been exploited to the last square foot. Yet engineers continue to do the impossible, driving four-lane highways through mountains and constructing immense concrete platforms up near-vertical slopes to create more building space.

While the urban concentrations of Hong Kong Island are now notorious, the beauties of the countryside are less well known. The visitor who ignores the south of the island misses some of the Colony's most spectacular views, some stunning walks, and countryside that combines subtropical vegetation and wild life with open scrub-land, some of it only a matter of minutes from Central.

Vistors to Hong Kong Island cannot expect to stumble across a Louvre or Westminster Abbey, but with little effort they can experience the island's extraordinary, intensely concentrated mix, surely unequalled anywhere else, of oriental and occidental, of urban and rural, of unsightly poverty and ostentatious wealth, of a nostalgic past and an aggressively modern present.

Central

The Central District of Victoria, usually simply known as Central, is the traditional heart of Hong Kong. It was the first area of the 'barren island' to be developed, and today is the centre of Hong Kong's commercial life. Behind concrete and reflecting glass thrives the colony's big business — finance, trade, banking. At lower levels elegant stores in air-conditioned shopping arcades serve a cosmopolitan clientele. During office hours, the whole area hums with aggressive activity; at night it empties.

There is much of Manhattan in Central's concentrated jumble of highrise blocks which grow almost visibly in a frenetic race to maximise land use. Down below ambitious crowds surge through the streets often spilling off pavements during lunch hour. The jostling pedestrian flow pauses only at windows displaying the latest stockmarket prices or at lengthy queues at the elevators that carry office staff back to work.

The first colonizers established in Central a pattern of rapid uncontrolled development that has barely been broken since. Within months of the British flag being raised in January 1841, a track along the coastline had become **Queen's Road** — still the district's main thoroughfare. European traders, including names familiar in Canton trading such as Jardine and Dent grabbed lumps of shoreline for their godowns (warehouses) and almost at once began to expand their territory by filling up sections of Victoria Harbour.

The reclamation process has continually altered the shape of the area ever since. By 1860 enough land had been reclaimed to build another waterfront road — **Des Voeux Road** — running parallel to Queen's Road. **Connaught Road** became the third parallel waterfront road in 1887, a pet project of Sir Paul Chater, the grand old man of Hong Kong real estate and the co-founder of the giant property developers Hongkong Land.

Few city centres can have experienced so many rapid changes in appearance as Central, where the tradition of tearing down buildings at short intervals to replace them with bigger ones, is deeply entrenched. Early photos of Des Voeux Road show elegant slightly Mediterranean 3-storey buildings with verandahs shaded by hanging bamboo blinds. Queen's Road had an exotic oriental look about it, packed with pigtailed men and rickshaws, flanked by colonnades of stores, the pillars strung with bold Chinese characters. (A few buildings in this style remain, in Queen's Road West).

Very few of the old buildings and little of the traditional Orient remain. Those buildings which have survived are in active use — there has been no place for sentimentality for the past. As incomes and exports increase, so do the scale of the buildings. To office workers today it must seem that construction sites, pneumatic drills and pile-drivers are a permanent fact of life.

Central's rich history exists in a less obvious way, not so much in the fabric of the buildings, but in the names of the streets, stores and buildings. **Pedder Street**, was called after Lt. W. Pedder, RN, a harbour master appointed by Captain Elliot. **D'Aguilar Street**, is named after Major-General D'Aguilar, the first Commander-in-Chief of the army in Hong Kong. Duddell was a notorious businessman, Pottinger the Colony's first governor, Captain William Caine, the first magistrate, Bonham, Bowring and Des Voeux all governors. **Ice House Street** of course contained the ice house, which operated twice daily delivery services of American-imported ice, and which collapsed in the 1880's when Hong Kong began to manufacture its own ice.

Some stores are also reminders of Central's early days. There is Lane Crawford, at first a ship's chandler, and now Hong Kong's classic Harrod's style department store. Watson's the Chemist goes back to the 1880's, as does Kelly and Walsh, the bookstore in Ice House Street, and publisher of early guidebooks to Hong Kong.

Central is linked to Kowloon by the **Star Ferry** (a subway leads down from Chater Road beside the Mandarin Hotel to the pier) and by the MTR. A bus terminus to the west of the Star Ferry is a convenient place to pick up buses for all parts of the island.

At the heart of Central is **Statue Square**, an open area cut into two unequal parts by Chater Road. The Square is virtually unrecognisable from the days when it was edged by ornate white-washed Colonial-style buildings, each topped with copulas and turretts and encircled by tiers of verandahs enclosed behind Corinthian columns and bulbous balustrades. The design of today's square, with its angular layout of covered sitting areas, rectangles of water and organised tree clusters, was finished in 1966. The square no longer acts as a showcase for imposing statues of British Royalty. Today there is only one statue — that of Sir Thomas Jackson who was chief manager of the Hong Kong and Shanghai Bank, 1876-1902. On the north side of Chater Road, a simple cenotaph commemorates the dead of both world wars.

The bravest expansion scheme recently carried out is that of the Hong Kong and Shanghai Bank, which has occupied the position on the southside of the square since 1865. Demolition of the good-looking '30's block that is familiar from millions of banknotes took place in the summer of 1981. But the building replacing these famous headquarters was designed to obliterate any momentary regrets with a dazzling display of steel and glass. Architectural correspondents and others say that British architects Foster Associates have given Hong Kong a much needed aesthetic treat with one of the world's most interesting and, at an estimated $1.4 billion, most expensive commercial developments.

With 47 levels above ground and four levels below ground, the bank's 600 feet high headquarters unquestionably dominates its banking neighbors. To the west is the **Chartered Bank**, another established international group. To the east is the chunky grey building of the **Bank of China**, its doorways guarded by solid square-faced Chinese lions. It is through this bank and a network of a dozen or so other China-controlled banks, that Peking holds sway over a sizeable proportion of Hong Kong's bank deposits (some say as high as 20%). Aside from its banking activities the building has doubled as Peking's trade, diplomatic and political headquarters. Anywhere else in the world the Bank of China's sombre presence would seem incongruous, with the Hilton behind it, the Hong Kong and Shanghai Bank next door, and a last remnant of Edwardian England, the Supreme Court Building, opposite. But in Hong Kong the peaceful proximity of such contasts is the norm.

On the east of Statue Square is the domed and colonnaded old Supreme Court, now under conversion into the home of the Legislative Council and the offices of the Unofficial Members of the Executive and Legislative Councils by the end of 1985. This typical piece of Edwardian public architecture (built 1903-11) was designed by Aston Webb, who was also responsible for London's Victoria and Albert Museum, the facade of Buckingham Palace and Admiralty Arch.

Walking a little way up Garden Road, past the Hilton, on the right hand side is the characteristically Victorian **St John's Cathedral** built between 1847-49, with a distinctive square neo-gothic tower. This is the oldest permanent centre of Christian worship in Hong Kong and still the focus of Hong Kong's Anglican Church. The first bishop was a missionary, George Smith, who was given a diocese which, with the supreme self — confidence of nineteenth century Britain, covered not only Hong Kong but also all of China and Japan. The ravages of white ants led to major restoration work in 1981.

A path from Garden Road leads past St John's Cathedral to a quieter green patch of mature trees and thick sub-tropical shrubbery. From here **Battery Path** slopes down to Queen's Road Central, past the red Amoy brick **Victorian District Courthouse**. The building, which dates back to the 1880s has a versatile past, housing at different times government departments, the Hong Kong and Shanghai Bank junior mess, Butterfield and Swire, the Russian Consulate and the French Mission.

The section of Queen's Road Central from Ice House Street to Pedder Street is dominated by massive construction activity — all part of giant property developers Hongkong Land's scheme for reshaping Central. Hongkong Land are masters of the art of acquiring, pulling down and putting up property in Central. But this plan exceeds all past efforts and includes covered walkways between their properties. It is now possible to walk from Battery Path to the MTR or Star Ferry without touching street level. The centre of this scheme is the **Landmark**, with its elegant window displays from the internationally chic. Eighty or so banks, airline offices, restaurants, jewellers and boutiques are housed here. Inside the Landmark, a vast air-conditioned hall incorporates the latest fashions in public indoor plazas. Escalators sail up, past murals, to suspended balconies; in a circular pool fountains shoot up higher when the noise level around increases; and above a kinetic glass fibre sculpture vibrates to light. At times the fountain in its high atrium is switched off, a platform erected over it and performances

Inside the Landmark

and displays mounted.

Crossing Connaught Road from Pedder Street, looking towards the harbour, the brand new 52-storey **Exchange Square** comes into view. It will house the new unified stock exchange and the Hong Kong Academy for Performing Arts by the end of 1985. Phase II of the project will be completed in 1988. Next to it is the massive round-windowed 52 storey **Connaught Centre** built in 1974. Both projects are owned by Hong Kong Land, and until the opening of the Hopewell Centre in Wan Chai, Connaught Centre was the tallest building in Hong Kong. Behind it is the General Post Office and Central's Government Publications Office, and to the east the Star Ferry pier. Beside the Star Ferry is a wide open promenade, Edinburgh Place, overlooking the harbour, with **City Hall**'s complex of buildings behind. Opened in 1962, these units are the focus of Hong Kong's public artistic life [see Arts]. The Low Block contains a concert hall, a theatre and two restaurants. The 12-storey High Block contains the Museum of Art [see Museums], an exhibition gallery and art gallery, libraries, lecture halls and the Hong Kong Marriage Registry (the garden below is a favourite spot for newly-weds to be photographed).

East of the City Hall complex is **HMS Tamar**, the Royal Navy shore base in Hong Kong. The British Armed Forces have always been a dominant presence in Central, and their insistance on retaining large chunks of land and shoreline was a long standing frustration to planners and developers. Today's base — sometimes known as the Stone Frigate, since it is officially classed as a Royal Navy Ship — is all that is left of the old Naval dockyard which before land reclamation stretched eastwards to Wanchai and right up to Victoria Barracks. The Army was housed in Victoria Barracks, first established in 1843. until 1978 when the headquarters moved in with the navy into the 28-storey Prince of Wales building in the HMS Tamar compound. The tower's narrow base is a security feature, which allows the entire building to be sealed off in an emergency.

Victoria Barracks is to be relocated, and a new 22-storey **Supreme Court Building** comprising a six storey podium and a 16-storey tower block housing 36 court rooms and ancillary accommodation was completed in 1984. The old Flagstaff House, now the **Flagstaff House Museum of Tea Ware**, is one of the finest remaining colonial buildings in Hong Kong.

Five minutes walk up from Queen's Road Central is **Government House**, the residence of the Governor. Entry is forbidden but it is possible to stare through the main gate in Upper Albert Road, at the sweeping drive and facade. The building started life as a square neo-classical structure, put up in 1855-6 under the watchful eye of Cleverly, a surveyor general of Hong Kong. Considerable alterations and additions have since been made, the most incongruous of which is the prominent quasi-oriental tower

constructed by the Japanese who occupied Government House during the Second World War. The Japanese were also responsible for lengthening the roof corners which are curved upwards and outwards, and for the portico.

One Sunday a year, in Spring when the garden's azaleas are in bloom, the grounds are opened up to the public. Queues form several hours before the gates open and the swarm of visitors detracts from getting an overall view of the building and grounds.

Opposite Government House are the **Botanical and Zoological Gardens**, well worth a visit for anyone seeking a pleasant sub-tropical leafy retreat. The tiny gardens were created on the terraced hillside in 1860, and since then the varied lush vegetation has made it one of Hong Kong residents' favourite promenades. If you go early in the morning you can watch people going through their *taichi* exercises. On a fine Sunday it is a place for family outings.

The small zoo boasts a fine collection of birds including the rare Palawan Peacock from the Philippines. The relatively small collection of mammals (orangutangs, monkeys, jaguars) still manages to attract more visitors than London Zoo — although entry here of course is free. You can enter from Garden Road, Albany Road, Glenealy or Robinson Road. The gardens are divided in two by Albany Road; an underground walkway links the two halves.

The Peak

As orientation for the first-time visitor to Hong Kong, or for the sheer delight of the views, nothing can beat the trip up to Hong Kong Island's highest mountain, Victoria Peak.

Since the 1870s when the Governor Sir Richard Macdonnell took to spending the hot and humid months in his summer residence on the Peak, the area has become the enclave of Hong Kong's rich and influential inhabitants. Many elegant houses are scattered over the slopes of Mount Kellet, Victoria Peak itself and Mount Gough, where the temperatures are lower but the social position is higher. Up here (said a 19th century traveller) 'one can spend the summer in Hong Kong with a reasonable probability of being alive at the end of it.'

In the early days access to the Peak was by sedan chair, but since 1888 the Peak Tram has taken much of the effort out of the 1300-foot, 8-minute climb. The number 15 bus from Central offers a longer (30-40 minutes) but no less scenic route to the top.

Public transport terminates at the **Peak Tower** which is in the saddle between the surrounding mountains. From the viewing platform or the restaurants there are splendid panoramic views of the northern shore of the island, across the harbour to Kowloon and Kai Tak Airport. In the opposite direction the southern side of Hong Kong Island comes into view across

Aberdeen to Lamma, Lantau and the South China Sea. Many fine walks begin from the Peak Tower complex. One of the easiest and most satisfying is the 45 minute stroll round Victoria Peak along Harlech Road and Lugard Road where the view changes every minute from Lamma, Lantau and other islands to an exciting bird's eye view of urban Hong Kong.

Western

For a taste of the traditional life of Hong Kong, there is no better place to go than Western — to the outsider an exotic, crowded district extending westward from Central that combines the picturesque with the apparently squalid. It is an old residential and commercial area of narrow streets of crumbling 3-storey buildings, hawkers' stalls and small wholesale outlets.

It was in Western that the British flag was first hoisted in January 1841. The event is commemorated by the name of a narrow, unprepossessing street **Possession Point** (not worth a special visit), and until recently by a small square surrounded by tumbledown houses. New highrise blocks and a covered hawkers' bazaar, painted in lurid turquoise, have now been put up in the square.

But there are still several chunks of Western to appeal to anyone looking for a glimpse of traditional urban Chinese life. Walk from Central or take a tram along Des Voeux Road to **Western Market**, an old building in deep red Amoy brick. Turn up into **Morrison Street**, part of an asymmetrical jumble of streets lined with fruit and vegetable stalls. On the left a herbalist sells two kinds of invigorating herbal drinks — one dark and bitter and the other light and sweet. On the corner with **Bonham Strand**, several shops sell traditional everyday wood, rattan and bamboo ware — ginger graters, rattan pillars, wok brushes, fans and washboards. This is the area for snake shops. At No 91 Bonham Strand the snakes are kept in smart wooden boxes, fitted ceiling to floor, with red and gold plush. No 127 is more down-market, with snakes quite visible in wire cages. In **Mercier Street**, amidst sellers of fishing tackle, string and tropical fish, is the Chinese Gold and Silver Exchange — a small insignificant looking building which does not permit spectators in, although even a glimpse through the door gives a lasting impression of the frenetic activity inside.

Further west towards **Sai Ying Pun**, the banks and general stores of Des Voeux Road give way to ship chandlers and dried foods wholesalers and retailers selling a bewildering array of dried fish imported from China, Japan and Korea. There are shark's fins of all qualities, the best of it often kept behind glass and priced at over $500 a catty (about 1¼lbs). Some of the dried merchandise is recognizable — whole fish, shrimps, oysters, snake (hung in large single coils), and squid. Others are less so. The brown one-inch discs in jars, for instance, are pieces cut from a scallop's root muscle and the yellowish papery squares are jelly fish with tentacles removed.

72

*Shelley Street Mosque above Caine Road, was the first
founded in Hong Kong. The present structure dates from 1916.*

Other stores specialize in dried mushrooms, including an expensive crinkly off-white fungus which expands dramatically when soaked and is good for a clear complexion, and the popular 'cloud ear' which looks like scraps of charred paper until it is cooked, when it takes on an elephant ear shape. Sacks of tangerine peel, red-brown melon seeds, dried lotus seeds, preserved bean-curd and much else also turn up in these shops.

Moving inland from here up **Centre** or **Eastern Street**, across Queen's Road West, the streets become very busy with markets selling Chinese vegetables, herbs, fruit, sweets, chickens and quails. At right angles First, Second and Third streets are characteristic of old residential Western, the houses adorned with a tangle of curved wrought iron balconies, pot plants, shrines, washing, wire-netting and bird cages.

Back eastwards a few blocks, the tiny streets around **Tai Ping Shan**, (north of Hollywood Road) are interesting. This area was the site of a Chinese settlement before Hong Kong was ceded to the British (Tai Ping Shan, or Mountain of Peace was the Chinese name for Victoria Peak). The early settlers were said to be followers of a notorious pirate, who controlled the waters around Hong Kong at the end of the eighteenth century. Later, when the number of Chinese immigrants increased as the British settled in, the area became an important densely populated, highly unhealthy commercial and residential centre. The original buildings were torn down at the end of the century after a particularly bad bubonic plague epidemic and rebuilt, but many of today's houses seem little altered from that period.

There are three small temples in **Tai Ping Shan Street**. The surrounding steep lanes, narrow alleyways and steps paved with smooth stones, are a mass of accompanying paraphernalia — joss-sticks, paper offerings to be burnt, and fortune tellers. On the corner with Pound Lane are the **Temples of Kuan-yin** and **Sui-tsing Paak**, their origins going back to 1840. Women whose children are ill, or who have other domestic problems flock to Kuan-yin. The general Sui-tsing Paak next door is believed to cure sickness. Several other gods are included in this temple, Tin Hau, the sea-goddess among them. An interesting hall has 60 images, each dedicated to one year of the Chinese dating system. Another has a replica of the mummified body of Hui Neng, founder of the Buddhist Vegetarian Sect. Outside is a much used open shrine to Earth Gods, who protect the local community. The third temple is the **Paak Sing**, first established in 1851 (and rebuilt in 1895), to keep tablets dedicated to the dead. The inner room contains over 3000 tablets (and photographs) of the dead. Temple keepers burn incense and oil lamps in front of the tablets for a small fee.

Walking back towards Central you come across Hong Kong's famous ladder streets. The Cantonese equivalent of 'stair street' is in fact more appropriate for these narrow steep stone staircases. The most spectacular is **Ladder Street**, which climbs 213 feet up from its junction with Hollywood

Road to Caine Road. There is a considerably shorter equivalent in Central
— Pottinger Street — lined with sellers of buttons and bows, sewing
cottons, shoes, combs and other haberdashery.

Hollywood Road and **Cat Street** (Upper Lascar Road) have lost
much of their character under an urban renewal scheme (though not their
antique shops nor Cat Street's flea market). The **Man Mo Temple** at No
126 — a fine example of a Taoist temple built on traditional lines — is well
worth a visit if you are in the area. It is heavily used by worshippers who
carry on apparently oblivious to the large number of tourists who go there.
The temple is dedicated to two Taoist deities — Man Cheong, the god of
literature who also looks after civil servants, and Mo Kwan Kung, the
martial god — who, it is said, represents the qualities of the two influential
Chinese community leaders who founded the temple in 1842. It was rebuilt
in 1894.

Behind the fire screening door at the main entrance, the atmosphere is
thick with smoke from the giant incense coils that hang in profusion from
the ceiling of the section known as 'the smoke tower'. The coils which burn
for two weeks are ideal for long term offerings. Written on the red tag that
hangs from each are the worshippers' prayers. Below, paper offerings are
burnt in the two stone incinerators and, on the other side, stand symbols of
the Eight Immortals.

On the long marble-topped table at the top of the steps that lead to the
main section (or palace) are two solid brass deer standing about three-feet
high, symbolizing long life. And on the table in front of the main altar are a
fine set of pewter Ng Kung, or five ritual vessels, as well as a central incense
burner, a pair of vases and candlesticks on either side.

On the main shrine Man Cheong (on the left) and Kwan Kung (on the
right) sit together. To the right is the shrine to the City God, Shing Wang,
who looks after city dwellers, and to the left is Pao Kung, the God of
Justice. The temple was in fact used early on as a Chinese Court to judge
disputes amongst the Chinese community. Also in the temple are three
finely carved, teak sedan chairs, which until recently used to carry the
statues of Man and Mo through the street during festivals. The temple drum
and bell (cast in Canton in 1847) are on the right hand wall. In the
adjoining All Saints Temple there is a soothsayer ready to tell you what the
gods have in store for you after shaking the chim.

Wanchai

Wanchai is associated in most people's minds with Suzy Wong, seamen,
and neon-lit nightlife [see Nightlife]. But for anyone prepared to explore on
foot, there is far more to this interesting old district, one of the five original
wan, the areas set aside for the Chinese population who arrived on Hong
Kong Island during the 1850s.

Wanchai was once a stretch of waterfront along Queen's Road East, but early this century reclamation provided new space for Wanchai's characteristic three- and four-storey tenements, with ground floor stores and residential quarters above, that spread as far as Gloucester Road, the 1930s waterline. Today there is another broad strip of reclaimed land on the north side of Gloucester Road, which is gradually filling up with new highrise office blocks, a sportsground, the Arts Centre [see Arts] and a ferry pier.

The face of pre-war Wanchai is rapidly disappearing as developers take over in a frenzy of office block construction. The highest of these (in fact the highest in Asia outside of Japan) is the **Hopewell Centre** which grows an improbable 64 storeys out of this crowded section of Queen's Road East. Apart from restaurants on floors 6-8, the revolving restaurant on top and two shopping floors, the whole cylindrical building is office space — a daring venture by a local developer, born and bred in Wanchai, which has resoundingly paid off.

Almost next door to the Hopewell Centre, in one of Wanchai's most enjoyable incongruities, is the single-storeyed **Hung Shing Temple** dedicated to a god of seafarers. A shrine inside is dated 1847-48, although the building was constructed in 1860. The splendid line of Shekwan pottery decorating the roof was added at the turn of the century. On the other side of the Hopewell Centre a picturesque alley, its name, Tik Loong Lane written over the entrance, leads up steps to a crumbling terrace of nineteenth century houses. Several of these incorporate the **Sui Pak Temple**, which was probably founded in the 1870s and is especially popular with people wanting medical help. The interior contains many mirrors inscribed by grateful worshippers who have recovered from illnesses. Upstairs is an interesting collection of antiques.

In the narrow side streets that lead into Queen's Road East you may stumble over traditional shops selling birds, crickets, snakes, or fragile brightly coloured paper offerings. Tiny workshops spill out onto the pavements, and on one or two corners professional letter-writers set up their desks. **Wanchai market**, which runs from Queen's Road East down Wanchai Road is one of the most interesting to wander through (go around 9-11am, or late afternoon).

Happy Valley

Racing began in Happy Valley in 1845 and has been one of the major preoccupations for Chinese and expatriates ever since [see Sports]. The height of enthusiasm was perhaps reached when Governor Sir Henry May, a keen horse-owner, took to the track as a jockey with some success.

Aside from the racecourse, Happy Valley, once swampy and malaria-ridden, is now a pleasant residential area, first becoming fashionable in the 1870s when the wealthy began to move away from Central. On the south

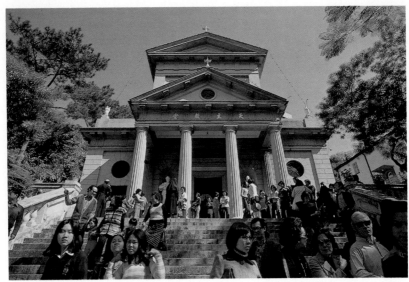

Catholic church, Happy Valley

side of the racetrack is an entrance to Happy Valley's **Colonial Cemetery** established in 1845. There is another entrance much higher on Stubbs Road. Amidst flowering trees and well-kept hillside gardens (the setting for a key scene in John Le Carré's *The Honourable Schoolboy*), the gravestones vividly summarize much of Hong Kong's early history. There are graves bearing British, Russian, German, and Chinese names. The many monuments include one to some American officers and crew who died in a boat attack on a fleet of piratical junks in 1855, one in memory of a French crew which disappeared in a typhoon in 1906 and of course many British soldiers and their families who died of fever. The new Aberdeen Tunnel emerges nearby.

Causeway Bay

Wanchai merges imperceptibly into Causeway Bay, the busy area most favoured by locals for shopping and eating. Innumerable restaurants, jewellers, camera shops, boutiques, and electrical stores mingle with the smartest China Products store in Hong Kong, three big Japanese department stores, a sleek new branch of Lane Crawford, and several shopping malls including Yee Tung Village specializing in traditional arts and crafts in the Excelsior Hotel. Prices throughout are better than in Central; hours are longer: shops are open from 10am to 9 or 10pm.

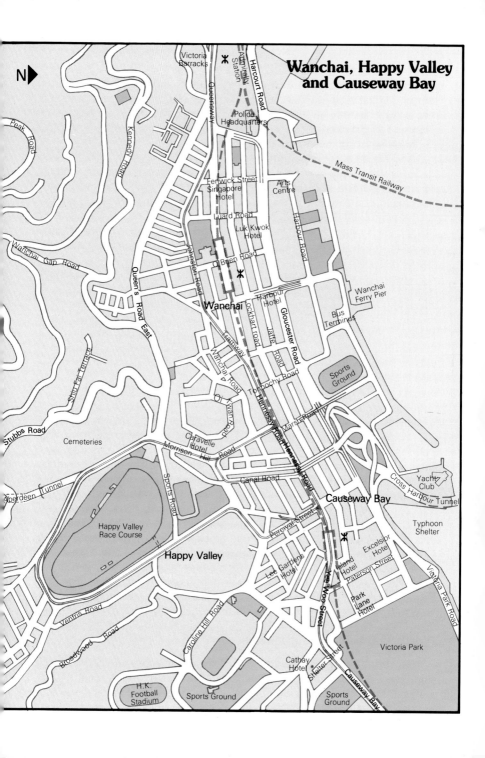

Trading is not new to Causeway Bay. The most famous *hong*, (trading house) Jardine Matheson, set up shop here in 1841. Jardine's most famous relic is the noon-day gun, made known to the world by Noel Coward's *Mad Dogs and Englishmen*:

'In Hong Kong they strike a gong
'And fire off a noonday gun.'

Extensive reclamation long ago lost Causeway Bay its bay, although it still has a **typhoon shelter**, where on summer nights (between April and November) you can hire a sampan on the waterfront (most easily reached via the pedestrian bridge from Victoria Park). The sampan will take you out into the shelter for a floating dinner. The food (not cheap) is chosen from the boats that cluster round the sampan, and a music boat will serenade you for extra dollars.

One bonus of reclamation done some 30 years ago was **Victoria Park**, opened in 1957. The 19 acre park is not especially beautiful but is an interesting and accessible place for an insight into Hong Kong's early morning life. (Between 6am and 7.30 is the best time to go.) Under clumps of trees, small unselfconscious groups of people of all ages go slowly through their *tai chi chuan* exercises. Impressively fit individuals practise various forms of kung fu while others jog round the flat central grass area. Bird cages are hung in the trees to give the birds an airing while their owners chat below. The park is heavily used throughout the day. It has swimming pools, mini-soccer pitches, tennis and basket ball courts, but has recently lost some land to the MTR for the construction of a new station.

A bizarre park of another kind is **Tiger Balm Gardens**, much maligned but a fascinating comment on Buddhist mythology and Chinese taste. These days it is usually full of Japanese tourists. The founder was Chinese millionaire philanthropist Aw Boon Haw who made his money with the most famous of cure-alls, Tiger Balm, which relieves asthma, lumbago, sore throat, scorpion bite and much else with equal success.

The garden was built in 1935 on eight acres of very steep hillside behind Causeway Bay. Grotesque and amusing plaster figures depicting Chinese folktales or Buddhist stories ornament every ledge and corner. Most lurid (and furthest to climb) are those presenting the ten Courts of Hell. There is also a monument to Aw's parents and a decorative Tiger Pagoda, with 149 steps up its six storeys. The gardens are open daily from 9am to 4pm.

North Point and Shaukeiwan

East from Causeway Bay to North Point, Quarry Bay and Shaukeiwan, population density and industry intensify. These areas are for anyone who wants to see something of Hong Kong's industrial life or low cost housing estates. **North Point**, or 'little Shanghai' because of all the Shanghainese who have settled there, is an oppressive mass of 1960s residential blocks, vast restaurants, streets markets and heavy traffic.

Quarry Bay is the oldest industrial area in Hong Kong — ship building began here with the establishment of Whampoa Dock in 1863. The Taikoo Dockyard, founded by Butterfield and Swire, was in full operation in 1908. Today much of it has been redeveloped as a large private housing estate — Taikoo Shing — while the remaining yards are operated by a joint concern, the Hong Kong United Dockyard Company.

Shaukeiwan was for a long time a small fishing village, persistently bothered by pirates, the most notorious of whom was based on the mainland opposite at Lei Yu Mun. This is the shortest stretch of water to the mainland, and the one the Japanese used when invading Hong Kong Island. Today the crossing can be made by public ferry to eat at one of Lei Yu Mun's seafood restaurants [see New Territories].

Shaukeiwan today is the base of Hong Kong's second largest fishing fleet (Aberdeen's is bigger), and a densely populated residential area. The traditional art of junk building carries on in **Aldrich Bay**, but there is much new industry as well. If you have time to spare, visit the **Tin Hau Temple** opposite the Fish Market, or the interesting **Tam Kung Temple**. Tam Kung, with his ability to heal the sick and control the weather, became the second-ranking patron deity after Tin Hau for boat people. His festival, on the 8th day of the 4th moon, is one of the island's most spectacular celebrations. Boats carrying shrines come from all over Hong Kong, offerings are made, and dragon and lion dances performed.

Repulse Bay and Stanley

No perspective of Hong Kong Island would be complete without making the easy trip to the south side of the island. Until 1920 when a road to Repulse Bay was completed, the fishing settlements at Repulse Bay and Stanley were small and isolated, accessible only on a narrow track, or by boat. Today there is a constant stream of traffic to these now popular residential areas, with regular buses and plenty of taxis. The route along Stubbs Road and Wongneichong Gap Road winds above Happy Valley race course, and crosses over to the greener side of the island. The road curls down steep slopes past smart houses and residential blocks in leafy settings, with superb views across to **Deep Water Bay** (where there is a pleasant though crowded beach), Ocean Park and Lamma Island. In off-peak traffic it takes half an hour from Central to Repulse Bay and another ten minutes on to Stanley.

The sandy shallow **Repulse Bay**, got its name from 19th-century pirate-chaser, the HMS Repulse. For some the name has strong colonial associations, largely because of the famous old **Repulse Bay Hotel** which was built in 1918 and has sadly been demolished. Without the hotel's

gracious open verandah, long a favourite place for afternoon tea or dinner under the twirling ceiling fans, there is little reason to stop off at Repulse Bay. The beach in front of the hotel, being the island's most accessible, is also its most heavily used.

Repulse Bay

The road through Repulse Bay winds on towards **Stanley**, passing more glorious views, and more up-market residences. Stanley had the largest population (some 2000 people) of any settlement on the island when the British arrived in 1841, but did not develop until the 1920s when the island road reached it. The village has strong military associations. Part of the headland, first set aside for army use in the 1930's, is still a restricted army base. Stanley was the scene of the most heroic, and inevitably hopeless, resistance to the Japanese invasion in December 1941, and it was here that Hong Kong's civilians were herded together in a camp, now Stanley Prison, until the Japanese surrender in August 1945.

Most visitors to Stanley these days are in search of bargains in the small **market.** Here bundles of jeans stacked unceremoniously on small stalls and sold at ridiculously low prices, take all the glamour out of the designers' names. Small rattan and porcelain shops cater increasingly for tourists, whose recent presence has led to a rise in prices, and a general smartening up of the narrow pedestrian market street swamped with merchandise.

Yet despite the tourist influx, Stanley village is still a pleasant place to spend a couple of hours. If you go by bus, get off at the small grassy triangle and walk down Stanley Market Street which slopes towards the fruit and vegetable market. On the right is a small **fish market** (best in the morning) and food stalls which cook the fish you buy for yourself in the market. For the market (where there is a Chinese Products shop) turn left off Market Street. If you feel like a swim, **Stanley's main beach**, facing Tai Tam Bay, is five minutes away back past the bus stop. There is also an interesting **Tin Hau Temple** at the other end of the village, thought to be around 200 years old and so the oldest on the island. Turn right at the bottom of Stanley Market Road into Stanley Main Street and walk along the promenade past the squatter huts to the temple where Tin Hau, the Queen of Heaven and guardian of all connected with the sea, stands looking out across the ocean.

The unpretentious temple has much in common with Hong Kong's other Tin Hau temples. But one unusual feature is the stone ledge four feet high, which runs round three walls of the main hall, carrying an awesome array of black and gold gods thought to date back some 200 years. Look out also, on the wall to the left of the altar, for the dirty skin of a tiger said to have been shot only a hundred yards from the temple by Japanese soldiers during the occupation of Hong Kong.

Shek-O

Shek-O, although today largely a commuter society, still has the air of an unkempt Cantonese village about it, in spite of countrified surroundings which include a large golf course and even a few vegetable farms. It is not easily accessible from Central: take a no. 9 from Shaukeiwan (about 30 minutes) or a taxi from Central (off-peak 50 minutes). At weekends the village attracts large crowds, but on week days the wide sandy beach is emptier and a walk through the warren of narrow pedestrian streets, around a tiny Tin Hau temple gives a glimpse of a lifestyle far removed from dense urban living on the island's north shore. Good plain Cantonese food is served in several simple restaurants. Walk through the village, along the main street to reach Shek-O headland, bordered by luxury houses, and down by a footbridge across to the tiny rocky island of Tin Tau Chau. In 10 minutes you can climb up the cemented path to a lookout position with splendid views north to Joss House Bay and the mainland, and south to Stanley Peninsula with a satellite communications station at its tip, and the Po Toi island group in the distance.

Ocean Park

Around 2 million visitors a year flock to Ocean Park, understandably one of the most popular places for Hong Kong families to spend a morning or an afternoon. After more than 10 years of feasibility studies and construction, Ocean Park was opened in January 1977. The 160 acre park is set in rocky terrain just east of Aberdeen and is split into a lowland and a headland area, linked by cable car. The low land area is now the site of Asia's first water playpark, Water World, which has giant slides, a wave pool, a rapids ride, and a toddlers' pool. The playpark adds further variety to the lowland area's already extensive attractions, including a zoo, children's playground, goldfish exhibition, dolphin feeding pools and a garden theatre where regular entertainment is given by sea lions and other animals and in the plaza area, by trained cockatoos and macaws.

But it is the spectacular 7-minute cable car ride to the headland in tiny continually moving bubbles high above the rocky slopes that makes the visit worthwhile. The views of Hong Kong's islands and the South China Sea are awe-inspiring. On the headland itself is the world's largest marine mammal tank and the world's largest aquarium. The Ocean Theatre with its panoramic backdrop holds 4000 people and stages performances by dolphins, sea-lions and a killer whale. The bilingual master of ceremonies is remarkable.

The vast Atoll Reef, a seawater aquarium, holds 200 different species of fish which swim around in an enormous tank that has been designed to give the impression of a coral reef. Viewing galleries take the visitor down from the shallow upper reef levels to depths normally reserved for deep sea divers. A Wave Cove with 328 feet of 'coastline' and a unique wave-making machine is a splendid home for sea-lions, seals and penguins which can also be viewed from an underwater gallery.

The southern end of the Aberdeen Tunnel is located opposite the entrance to Ocean Park.

Aberdeen

The old fishing town of Aberdeen has tradionally been included on the Hong Kong Island tourist route. But recent changes have been so sweeping that many visitors feel it is hardly worth a special visit. The area is fast developing into an urban-industrial district to equal North Quarry Bay and Shaukeiwan. Reclamation of the harbour has all but destroyed the old character of the waterfront, although, apparently undeterred, the boat people still sell their fresh catch to passers-by and noisy sampan ladies tout for custom. The famous floating restaurants were moved away from the waterfront in 1978 to less spectacular moorings in a secluded part of the typhoon anchorage. On shore, the centre of the town is now a western-

View from Ocean Park

style shopping complex surrounded by highrise resettlement blocks.

But still an extraordinary sight is Aberdeen's crowded typhoon shelter. The splendid natural harbour, protected by the island of Ap Lei Chau, served as an anchorage for early voyagers to China long before the British arrived in Hong Kong. Today it houses the largest community of boat people in Hong Kong. A sampan from the waterfront will take tourists for a ride through the congested harbour, giving a close-up view of the boat people's life, which is mostly played out very publicly on the open decks. Sampan ladies are quick to seek out visitors, but less quick to agree on a reasonable price for the tour.

For a fine overview of the harbour you can climb up some steps onto the Ap Lei Chau Bridge pedestrian walkway. The bridge, opened in 1979, allowed the twentieth century to spill onto this tiny island, which had existed earlier entirely on its flourishing ship-building industry.

For shipbuilding enthusiasts, the shipyards around Ap Lei Chau are a paradise. Many kinds of small craft are built here including, of course, junks, which are still constructed by skilled carpenters who today have added electric drills to their traditional tool kits. Diesel engines, which have replaced the picturesque sails, are repaired here. Scrap iron and steel from ships broken up here is converted into metal products used in the construction industry.

The disfiguring five-chimney electric power station that dominates the

Sunset, St. Stephens Beach, Stanley

island provides power for much of Hong Kong Island.

Because of the large boat population, Aberdeen's Tin Hau Temple is heavily used. It was built in 1851 on what was then the shoreline, but today it is in the centre of town set in a small garden. The bell on the left as you enter the temple was made in 1726 and supposedly dredged up from the sea by local fishermen. The one on the right dates from 1851. Tin Hau sits in the central shrine with a smaller image of herself in front (this is carried out of the temple at festivals). Two almost life-sized generals stand in front of her — Thousand-Li Eye on the left, who could see a thousand li (300 miles), and Favourable Wind Ear on the right, who could hear distinctly up to a thousand li away. To Tin Hau's left and right are shrines to Pi Tai who fought the demon king bare-footed and wearing a black robe.

Kowloon

Little is known of Kowloon's early history, though the Lei Cheng Uk tomb [see Museums] in Lai Chi Kok (just north of Kowloon) is evidence of Eastern Han Dynasty (25-220AD) settlers. In 1277 the Sung Dynasty's last emperor Ti Ping and his brother Ti Ching, under the guardianship of their uncle Yang Liang-Chieh, found refuge in Kowloon. The Mongol army from which they were fleeing had captured and disposed of their eldest brother, the former emperor, and taken the Southern Dynasty's capital of Hangchow. On arrival in Kowloon a temporary court was set up near the present airport. Here the eight-year old emperor and his brother are said to have spent many hours playing in the shadow of a great rock overlooking the sea. Some years later the rock was engraved with the message 'Sung Wong Toi' (Terrace of the Sung Emperor). Sadly during the Japanese Occupation in the Second World War it was broken up to make way for the Kai Tak runway, though the fragment bearing the inscription was saved and can be seen today in the **Sung Wong Toi Garden**.

On his arrival the young emperor asked the name of his new home, and was told that it was Kowloon, meaning 'nine dragons' after the surrounding hills. (It was believed that dragons lived along mountain ridges.) When he remarked that there were only eight — today there are fewer as some have fallen foul of the developers' dynamite — he was told that he, the emperor was the ninth. (The dragon was a symbol of majesty.)

The next major event in Kowloon's recorded history was its cession in 1860 to Britain at the end of the Second Opium War. In 1895 Kowloon was described by Henry Norman, a traveller, as the 'ground floor' of the colony, Mid-levels being the 'second storey' and the Peak the 'top storey'. In other words Kowloon was one of the mercantile centres, Mid-levels was executive living, with the Peak for the *taipans* (bosses). This is very much the feeling of Kowloon today — a bustling market place. Indeed again to quote Mr Norman it 'just hums'.

The Kowloon Peninsula is surrounded by one of the most breathtaking and vibrant scenes in the world — **Victoria Harbour**. With the startling backdrop of mountainous Hong Kong (Victoria) Island with its multitude of buildings, some climbing precariously up to the Peak, this perfect natural harbour of 23 square miles is a constant hive of activity. It plays host to all manner of craft — aged junks from the mainland propelled majestically by great patched sails; jetfoils and hydrofoils plying between Hong Kong and Macau; the more sedate lozenge-shaped Star ferries; sleek warships; container vessels and bulk cargo carriers; tugs and lighters; police launches and every imaginable type of pleasure vessel. Once a year the liner Queen Elizabeth II docks at Ocean Terminal. Surprisingly amid this active scene you are likely to see a solitary sampan violently bobbing up and down, its

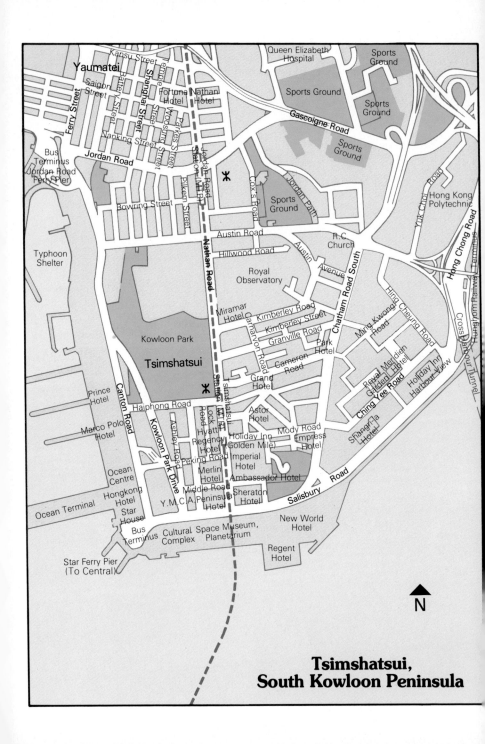

Tsimshatsui,
South Kowloon Peninsula

occupant fishing calmly. In 1842 a total of 381 vessels used the harbour: in 1980 the figure was 55,315. Harbour watching, a constant pleasure whether from land or sea, will be enhanced by the completion in 1981 of a walkway along the waterfront from Kowloon Pier to Hunghom. A night-time crossing on the Star Ferry is particularly spectacular. If you miss the last ferry home (11.30pm) hire a walla-walla from Blake or Queen's Pier: on one of these small noisy water taxis you will find yourself caught up in the true fairy-like quality of the harbour at night.

The area of the Kowloon Peninsula is 4.3 square miles stretching north from the waterfront to Boundary Street which marks the extent of the land ceded in 1860. Tsimshatsui which means 'sharp sand point' (a tongue twister pronounced Chim Sa Choy) is the peninsula's town. Surprisingly many of the neighbouring districts such as Laichikok and the **Walled City of Kowloon** are strictly speaking not in Kowloon proper. The so-called Walled City was built in the 1840s by a group of Chinese who wished to protect themselves from the British 'barbarians'. The walls, like Sung Wong Toi, disappeared when during the Second World War occupation the Japanese needed stones to build the Kai Tak runway, so today little remains of the old city.

The best way to see the southern part of Tsimshatsui is on foot. If you arrive by Star Ferry, just prior to docking you will see on the right a fine pink and white clock tower built in 1910. This is all that remains of the old railway station which was demolished in 1978 to make way for the Cultural Complex. **The Clock Tower**, protected from the wreckers' hammer, has caused certain amusement in the past, by sometimes working backwards. Just to the left of the Star Ferry exit are the vast shopping complexes of **Ocean Terminal and Ocean Centre** [see Shopping]. In addition to the cornucopia of shops and restaurants, on Wednesday evenings (between 6-7pm) the HKTA produces an interesting Cultural Show in the main hall of Ocean Terminal.

Walking along Salisbury Road, in the first block on the left (opposite the bus station) is Star House. Here on the ground and first floors is the largest and best stocked **Chinese Arts and Crafts Store** [see Shopping]. On the second floor is the **Chinese Export Commodities Exhibition Hall**, which is mainland China's showcase for displays of archaeological treasures, or products ranging from tractors to exquisite silk embroidery. Often there are visiting craftsmen demonstrating how handicraft items are made in different provinces.

Leaving Star House continue walking east past the imposing portico of the **YMCA**. On the opposite side of the street is the **Space Museum** and site of the **Cultural Complex** [see Museums]. Walking further along Salisbury Road you pass the venerable Peninsula Hotel [see Hotels]. Turn left up **Nathan Road**, main artery of Kowloon. This three mile tree-lined boulevard was built at the turn of the century during the governorship of Sir Mathew Nathan. At the time sceptics dubbed it Nathan's Folly: what possible use, they asked, could this boulevard serve in a sparsely populated unfashionable area? However, times have changed and the southernmost mile is a densely populated, highly commercial area (surveys point to this being shoppers' prime beat). The streets to right and left offer a host of diversions, in fact nearly anything anyone could desire [see Shopping and Nightlife].

Sung Dynasty Village

One of the newer sights (opened in 1979) in Kowloon is a replica of a **Sung Dynasty** (960-1279AD) **Village**. Traditionally Chinese architects, notably garden architects, have dealt with small spaces very cunningly, only allowing the visitor to see small sections of a whole area at any one time, thereby creating the illusion that it is much bigger than it is. To some extent this 60,000 square feet village follows this concept. The overall plan is a rectangle edged with buildings and a picturesque stream bordered by open fronted shops and mature trees meandering through the central space. Once inside the great entrance gate the tour begins in earnest. First comes a monkey show, then a look at the contemporary weapons on display in the village tower, followed by calls at the quaint stream-side shops where, with the help of the Sung paper money coupons handed out on arrival, one can buy sesame seed cookies and a longed-for cup of jasmine tea while listening to musicians accompanying a young lady singing. All the villagers are in Sung costume, in which they seem quite at home, and use the available props well. Against a 'beauty's recline' — the slanted bench of a pavilion — lounges a comely maiden while others sing prettily from their canopied boat. In the village square itself a bride arrives in a red sedan chair, (traditionally the bridegroom's first glimpse of his bride was when, on alighting from her sedan chair, her veil was lifted). In summer it is a relief to reach the rich man's house: it is powerfully (and incongruously) air-conditioned and contains a number of interesting antiques. After that there is an excellent variety show — acrobats, dancers and a performance of martial arts. Then one can visit a fortune teller before repairing to the Restaurant of Plentiful Joy for a snack and some more music. The final exhibit is a large wax museum which includes a tableau of the boy Sung Emperor Ti Ching [see Museums] being carried on his uncle's back into the sea to drown, thus escaping capture by the invading Mongols.

The Sung Village is one of Hong Kong's most popular attractions. It has been well constructed with much attention to architectural detail — the project took 5 years and cost $15 million. The shop houses are more successful than the larger buildings which look rather too new and glossy. It is necessary to join a tour (costing between $105-$135), except on Saturday and Sunday when the shows are not put on and for $30 you can roam alone. There are four tours daily leaving by coach from six central points — your hotel will have details. Children love this tour.

When taking the dinner tour (which departs from the Furama Hotel at 4.20pm and Lee Gardens Hotel at 4.30pm), it is possible to combine a visit to the adjacent **Lai Chi Kok Amusement Park**. You will then have to take a taxi or bus back to your hotel. Apart from being a conventional fun fair with ferris wheels, candyfloss and so on, Chinese Opera is performed here every evening from 7-7.30pm. Another site well worth visiting in this area is the **Lei Cheung Uk Tomb and Museum** [see Museums].

The most practical method of visiting these attractions is by tour bus. But for a spot of adventure and a more direct experience of Hong Kong why not forsake this comfortable yet sterile mode of transport and make an expedition to some of the rest of Kowloon's most interesting sights by MTR and on foot? Take the MTR — an experience in itself — to **Wong Tai Sin** Station, and follow the signs to the temple right beside the station. This traditionally designed large new temple, opened in 1973, is a 'miu', in other words dedicated to several creeds — Taoist, Buddhist and Confucian in this case. It is one of Hong Kong's most popular and the crowds thronging it generate a sense of excitement. The site is in the midst of a concrete jungle of flats and is overlooked by the majestic Lion Rock which gives it excellent fung shui. (fung shui— literally meaning wind and water — is said to influence the pattern of people's lives both for good and evil. To achieve the best *fung shui* the site, whether of a religious or secular building, is chosen by a professional geomancer and must combine harmony of the elements and the celestial world.) Enter the temple through its main gate, paying the 10 cents entrance fee which goes to charity, past Lord Buddha's delightful small pagoda and on up to the terraces. Here the air buzzes with the shaking of *chim*. These are bamboo cylinders containing thin bamboo sticks; which are shaken until a stick drops out. The number on this stick corresponds to a message which is then bought from and interpreted by a soothsayer. Unlike most temples the inner sanctum is cordoned off and entry is left to the discretion of the gatekeeper. Inside it is very ornate, and in the centre of a huge gilt altar stands a portrait of the Taoist god Wong Tai Sin, who is thought to possess the power to heal. Many believers say that the water at his temple — though it comes straight from the tap — heals the

Yaumatei Typhoon Shelter

sick. Down one side of the temple runs an alley full of soothsayers' stalls, decorated with all manner of charts and gay red Chinese characters advising would-be clients of their talents.

The next stop on this expedition is the **Yaumatei Typhoon Shelter**. Take the MTR back to Waterloo Station, emerge at the Portland Street exits and then walk east three blocks. As you approach the last block on the left, you will hear a strange clack-clack noise. On inspection this old building turns out to be a wholesale fruit market: salesmen tout for business by clacking their mini abacuses like castanets.

Across the road is Yaumatei Typhoon Shelter. It was built in 1915 after a disastrous typhoon, and is today the home of hundreds of families. These boat people are made up of two groups, the Tanka and Hoklo. The Tanka (immortalised in many works by Chinnery) are said to be the indigenous fisher folk of the South China Sea while the Hoklo came later possibly from Fukien province. They speak different dialects and can also be told apart by their junks and distinctive head-gear (the Hoklo's reminiscent of Spanish style with a large horizontal brim, the Tanka's resembling a solar topee). The Tanka fish the deep waters and have larger vessels, whereas the Hoklo stick nearer in shore with their low gunwaled, high sterned craft.

Historically the boat people have suffered badly from discrimination. The Canton authorities used to refuse them the right to settle onshore, marry non-boat people or sit the civil service examinations, thereby excluding them from officialdom. In Hong Kong, they were barred from living onshore until 1911. Today these communities are shrinking as many of their young people, no longer victims of discrimination, prefer to live on land. However it is still fascinating to walk along the shelter: the community is totally self sufficient with its shop sampans, barbers, school, doctors and so on. Some of the older junks are magnificent and serve not only as the homes of several generations but also of their dogs, chickens and invariably a Tin Hau shrine [see Festivals] wherein a light continuously burns.

One block beyond the south end of the Shelter is Man Cheong Street, where a delicious smell of baking will make even the most disciplined nose twitch. Half way along this street of bakeries is Heyton which makes mouth-watering Chinese custard tarts and other delights for the peckish adventurer. Refreshed, cross Ferry Street, go along Kansu Street and there every morning between 10am and 4pm at the intersection with Battery Street you find the Jade Market.

The curb and pavement are covered with travelling salesmen's suitcases, with all sorts of jade objects — predominantly bangles and pendants. Some are displayed on gleaming white satin while others make do with crumpled newspaper. The more serious salesmen produce theirs in blue cloth boxes with white toggles. People are everywhere, browsing, haggling, and every now and then a small group gathers to examine a special piece. Serious sales are conducted silently with the aid of sign language, tic-tak style. (In Ching times interested parties would slip their hands inside each other's ample silk sleeves indicating their price by finger pressure.)

The Chinese regard for jade is perhaps best expressed by Confucius: 'it is soft, smooth and shining like kindness; it is hard, fine and strong, like intelligence; its edges seem sharp, but do not cut, like justice; it hangs down to the ground like humility; when struck, it gives a clear, ringing sound, like music; the stains in it which are not hidden and add to its beauty are like

Jade Market, Yaumatei

truthfulness; its brightness is like heaven, while its firm substance, born of mountains and the water, is like the earth.' In religious and domestic life jade has played an important role, as the early Chinese believed it held the elixir of life. During the Han Dynasty (206 BC-220 AD) the wealthy were buried in suits of jade. Some of the greatest treasures of the Ming and Ching Dynasties are of finely worked jade. Today many people, even small children, wear a piece of jade as a talisman. It is said to be difficult to pick up a true bargain at the jade market but you never know your luck.

At the intersection of Canton Road and Jordan Road is **King George V Memorial Park**. Early in the morning this is crowded with people practising *tai chi chuan*. When performed by an expert, these balletic movements are a pleasure to watch, the idea being not only to exercise the body but also to achieve harmony of body and mind. It is worth looking in the park as a late riser may still be exercising.

Walk along Jordan Road eastwards and turn right up Shanghai Street into a market area bustling with fascinating things to wonder at: slippery mounds of sea cucumbers — thought by some to be a delicacy — in pink buckets, neat squares of beancurd on thick wooden slabs, herbalist stalls, medicine shops emitting a strange yet nostril-clearing smell. Turn left into Bowring Street and find shop No. 36. This is hung from ceiling to floor with little bamboo bird cages, filled with birds of all sizes and colours, and even some crickets and squirrels. Outside the shop you may see a huge pile of

Herbal tea shop off Shanghai Street

small brown paper parcels. When unpacked more bamboo cages are revealed complete with charming blue and white porcelain food and water bowls.

You may be able to resist the temptation of stopping for a delicious *dim sum* lunch at Evergreen Restaurant, 136 Woosung Street or one of the many other restaurants in this small area. If so continue on eastwards along Bowring Street into Nathan Road and the Jordan MTR Station for your return to the modern world. Taken gently this meander around Kowloon will take you about four hours.

Two other localities in this part of Kowloon ought not to missed. As the expedition just described is enough for even the most hardened traveller in one go, why not make a separate expedition? For **Public Square Street** take the southernmost exit from the Waterloo MTR Station and walk two blocks south. Here you will find a temple complex, fortune tellers and public letter writers — a surprisingly, albeit shrinking, number of middle-aged Chinese are illiterate. Nearby in **Temple Street** Kun Wo Tung sells his famed turtle meat soup — a medicinal cure-all. At dusk this street, which in the old days was a favourite haunt of prostitutes turns into a colourful night market. For the **Bird Market** take the MTR to Argyle Station, go two blocks west and then left into Hong Lok Street. The birds in this truly fascinating spot are probably more pampered than the British dog. Nearby is Wan Loi Restaurant (484 Shanghai Street), a tea house especially furnished to accommodate the bird lover and his charge.

New Territories

Technically the New Territories include all of Hong Kong except Kowloon, Stonecutters Island and Hong Kong Island, but this section will deal only with the 281-square mile land mass which sprawls between the Chinese border and the Kowloon peninsula.

The New Territories acquired their name on 11 June 1898 when Britain signed a 99-year lease with the Chinese on the pretext of providing a line of defence for Hong Kong Island and Kowloon. As part of the same concession Britain secured sole trading rights up the River Yangzi thus protecting vital commercial interests from the ambitious French and Russians. Soon after this acquisition 'tales of its beauty and enchantment' wrote a British historian, 'were passed back across the Kowloon hills — tales of paved mountain paths, walled villages of the plain . . . . . silent bays and silver sand'. Much of this unspoilt magic can still be found, but today it co-exists with dense urbanization. Indeed the New Territories are undergoing one of the world's biggest urban development programmes. During the 1980s up to a third of Hong Kong's total population will be rehoused in a series of vast new towns — some with populations of as much as 500,000.

The schizophrenic character resulting from this transformation is exemplified by **Shatin** once a small seaside town of 40,000 inhabitants. It is said that the rice grown here was so succulent that it was sent north to the emperor's table. But today its harbour has been filled in (literally by bulldozing a hilltop into the water) and along with its surrounding fertile valley, is being transformed into a jungle of skyscrapers. But don't let this put you off, side by side with its concrete and steel Shatin offers plenty of cultural interest. Spectacularly sited in a bowl of jagged hills, it is an exciting first stop for a tour around the New Territories.

Shatin lies beyond the mountain range that protects Kowloon from the north. To get there by road drive through the **Lion Rock Tunnel**. You emerge below the **Amah Rock** (or Waiting for Husband rock), shaped like a mother carrying her child. One legend is that her husband, a bodyguard at the Sung court in Kowloon [See Kowloon], was killed after a battle against the Mongols. Every evening she would climb this hill and vainly await his return, until eventually the gods took pity, released her soul and turned her body into stone. The rock can best be seen prominently against the southern skyline from further down the Shatin valley.

Just before reaching Shatin is another memento of the past, a well-preserved walled village named **Shan La Wai**, 'walled village at the foot of hill'.

High up on the tree-clad hill, **Tao Fong Shan**, overlooking Shatin from the northwest, is the **Chinese Mission to Buddhists** (strange as it may seem a Lutheran organisation). In 1929 Karl Ludwig Reichelt, who had spent many years in China teaching Christianity to Buddhists, arrived in

Hong Kong in search of a perfect site for a proposed community. At Tao Fong Shan an expert in Chinese Buddhist architecture was employed and the foundations were laid in 1931. The resulting complex of buildings is delightful. One approaches the collection of whitewashed houses with blue roofs through an archway. The central building is a striking hexagonal chapel. A new guesthouse to accommodate 44 people has just been finished. There is a pottery decoration shop where the work is carried out by former Buddhist monks; the motifs are mostly religious but special orders are accepted. Throughout the compound are lovely plants and flowers and the view of Shatin valley is spectacular. There is no better place to spend two calm days if you can spare the time.

Ching Chung Koon Monastery Castle Peak

On the next hill stands the **Ten Thousand Buddha Monastery** with its hexagonal pink pagoda. It is reached by a stiff 500-step climb through a pine and bamboo wood — pretty except for the empty cans thrown everywhere. Round the walls of the main temple (built in 1950) are some 12,800 Buddhas of varying size. In front of the temple is the pink pagoda and to the right — a bizarre touch — a collection of children's fairground cars. If your tastes tend towards the macabre climb a little further up to the three temples above. Here you can see the embalmed body of the monastery's founder, the Reverend Yuet Kai. He died in 1965 aged 87 and, according to his wishes, was buried in a sitting position. Eight months later the body was exhumed and was said to be in perfect condition. It was

A remote village near the Chinese border

then covered in gold leaf and this diminutive figure now sits in a glass case on the altar. (The wisps of hair protruding through the gold from the chin are still said to grow.)

While in Shatin it is impossible to miss the imposing **Shatin racecourse** [see Sport]. Opened in 1978 this 250 acres of reclaimed land accommodates three tracks, stands for 37,000 racegoers, a central public park and a multitude of other buildings including a horses' swimming pool and air-conditioned stables. Next door is the site of the impressive **Jubilee Sports Centre** [see Sport] with several gyms and various sports facilities which opened in 1982.

Shatin boasts several delicious restaurants: **Luk Yuen** and **Lung Wah Hotel** which specialize in pigeon, and the **New Shatin**, famous for stuffed nightshade flowers. But for a real surprise go down a small steep track to the left of the main road descending from the Lion Rock Tunnel to the **Shatin Seafood Restaurant**. In addition to a menu of marine delicacies this obscure restaurant has one of the most distinguished wine lists (notably the first growth clarets) in Asia.

Continuing north from Shatin on the Taipo road you see the **Chinese University** — an imposing 1960s acropolis commanding views both over the Shatin valley and the serene lengths of the Tolo Harbour to the east. The University has some 4500 students. Unlike its sister Hong Kong University, the language of tuition is Chinese. Its museum [see Museum] is well worth a visit.

A little further on towards Taipo, built at the end of an isthmus, is **Island House**, the official residence of the Secretary of the New Territories. During the occupation it was used as the headquarters of the Japanese Commander of the New Territories. Stop on the road and contemplate the breathtaking view down Tolo Harbour — sparkling water, the occasional junk, the mountains receding in layers, so characteristic of Chinese landscape.

Before going down into Taipo itself turn off to **Taipo Kau**. Here there is a delightful rural English-style railway station and a ferry pier. Twice a day ferries leave for Tap Mun Island at the mouth of Tolo Harbour. The four-hour round trip, with stops at several islands and villages, affords an excellent glimpse of rural life. There are many permutations of this journey: the HKTA will give you all the timetables and advice needed. One can also get a ferry here for Ping Chau in Mirs Bay — not to be confused with Peng Chau, near Lantau — which is practically in Chinese territorial waters.

As early as the 8th century **Tolo Harbour** is known to have been a centre of the pearl fishing industry — in those days an extremely dangerous affair. The divers (who were Tanka people) were conscripted by the imperial household. They frequently had to be supervised by military guards both to ensure that they worked and to prevent smuggling. The fishing system is described in a Yuan Dynasty petition which brought about its abolition on humanitarian grounds; 'the method of gathering them is to tie stones onto a man and lower him into the sea so he will sink quickly. Sometimes he gets pearls and sometimes not. When he suffocates he pulls the rope and a man in the boat hauls it up. If this is done a fraction too late the man dies'.

Taipo itself, once a sleepy market is, like Shatin, undergoing a metamorphosis. A hundred and twenty acres are being reclaimed from its seashore to build an industrial estate alongside the remains of the old market town (the market itself still operates nine times each lunar month). In June, Taipo is one of the favourite venues for the Dragon Boat Festival [see Festivals]. On the road to Plover Cove Reservoir is a small 280-year old temple dedicated to Tin Hau, Goddess of the Sea.

Along the street is the marble-faced factory of the **Tai Ping Carpet Company**. Established in 1956 it is particularly proud of its list of 'prestigious installations', such as Buckingham Palace and the home of Bob Hope. On the floor below the plush showroom are the workshops. The workforce deftly inject row upon row of huge hanging canvases with wool from a gun-like machine. Several types of pile and non-pile carpets are produced in both traditional and modern designs. To see the workrooms ring 0-6565161 to make an appointment. On the waterfront stands a large architectural melange. This eccentric but rather marvellous Elizabethan Gothic folly, now deserted, is one of several remarkable buildings constructed by the Eu family.

Continue along the north side of Tolo Harbour to the **Plover Cove Reservoir**, these next few miles over the watershed and down into Starling Inlet are some of the most beautiful accessible by road in the New Territories. **Brides Pool**, a little way off the road and along a stream is a perfect picnic spot. In summer these hills are covered with flowers, wild gardenias, honeysuckle, rose myrtle — a flower and butterfly lover's dream.

Where the road joins Starling Inlet is the **Luk Keng Egretry**. From April to September this tree-clad hill is crowded with noisy egrets (small crane-like birds). Three species are indigenous to Hong Kong and they all (an estimated 800) nest here. One often sees these elegant birds standing in the paddy, or sometimes on the back of water buffalo. (The **Mai Po** marshes near Lok Ma Chau on the northwestern side of the New Territories, are excellent for birdwatching. To visit them it is necessary to obtain a permit from the Department of Agriculture and Fisheries; again the HKTA will help.)

Between Luk Keng and Fanling the land is intensely farmed, mostly with small neat squares of vegetable gardens. The farming methods are still old-fashioned, with night soil often the only fertilizer used. The farmers are predominantly elderly, the young prefering easier factory work. The women bending in the fields wearing crownless straw hats, black cloth hanging from the brim — like a horse's tail when swished it keeps the flies away — are Hakka people. The Territories' population is made up of four groups, the Punti who speak Cantonese, the Hakka with their own dialect and the two boat peoples [see Kowloon]. For those interested in architecture this area is rich in fine buildings including five walled villages (see the Government's excellent publication *Rural Architecture in Hong Kong*).

For a clear view of China go to Lok Ma Chau (Dismount Hill) border post. The legend is that the last Sung emperor, when fleeing from the Mongols, rested here, so those on the hill at the time had to dismount and kowtow in respect. The energetic can get an even clearer view by climbing up to **Robin's Nest** peak.

Crossing over to the western side of the New Territories you reach **Kam Tin** where there are three walled villages all built about 500 years ago. Among the settlers who arrived during the late Sung Dynasty were the five Great Clans. The Tangs, who were the earliest to arrive, chose the most fertile land and became the most powerful. To protect themselves against bandits these families surrounded their villages with sturdy walls. **Kat Hing Wai** is the best preserved and is geared up for tourists with trinket-covered souvenir stalls. It is more interesting to visit **Wing Lung Wai** and **Shui Tau Tsuen** particularly the latter's Ancestral Hall and Hung Shing Temple.

In the aftermath of the Chinese Communist Revolution (1949) many thousands of refugees poured into the New Territories with little or no money to restart their farming activities. The philanthropic Kadoorie brothers realised the need for agricultural education and set up the Kadoorie

Agricultural Aid Association. In the subsequent 30 years the project has snowballed: 1218 villages have received help; 199 miles of road and 254 bridges have been constructed making formerly inaccessible areas available for cultivation and, through research and husbandry courses at the **Kadoorie Experimental Farm** (near Tai Po), new farming methods have been accepted. It is possible to visit this 360 acre farm and garden (9.30am-4.30pm by appointment 0-981317). It has been beautifully landscaped, with both exotic and native trees blooming in profusion.

Vast piles of empty oyster shells herald the proximity of the fishing village of **Lau Fau Shan.** These oysters are either dried or made into oyster sauce rather than eaten raw. Situated on Deep Bay, the village is within a stone's throw of the mainland. Indeed it is across this stretch of water that many refugees attempt to swim. Seafood auctions are held every day in the main street, and the **Sun Tao Yuen Restaurant** provides all manner of seafood including, of course, oysters.

To the south-west of the New Territories are three interesting monasteries. **Castle Peak Monastery**, is steeped in history. It stands high on Tsing Shan (Green Mountain) overlooking Tuen Mun New Town and long-since silted up Castle Peak Bay. This bay was the staging post for ships trading in and out of China — the pearls from Tolo Harbour were probably brought overland and shipped from here. Tuen Mun means 'garrisoned entrance' and the foundations of a fort believed to date from 750 AD have been found near the monastery. The monastery was founded, tradition says, by an eccentric-sounding Buddhist monk named Pei Tu (literally 'cup ferry' referring to the wooden bowl he carried around which apparently he used to cross water). There is a stone image of Pei Tu in a dark cove above the monastery where he used to meditate. A military commander is said to have put it here in his honour in 964 AD. During the following centuries the monastery prospered, was rebuilt several times, and at one time was taken over for a short spell by the Taoists. Today it is inhabited by two Buddhist monks and three followers. The delightful complex of buildings includes a large, slightly tilting, restaurant which serves vegetarian meals. This leads onto a spacious terrace backed with 'evening fragrance' bushes, their exquisite smell not just confined to the evening. The stunning view was beautifully described by Confucian scholar Han Yue (820 AD) who 'looked over the vast unfathomable ocean and the forests and water and felt that it was indeed a sacred spot'. Another of the monastery's treasures is the '10,000 year old bone of a dragon' which is housed in a cage under an ancient gnarled tree literally balancing on its roots. If possible visit this outstanding monastery with a Mandarin speaker. The abbot has a wealth of historic anecdotes.

Some early foundations from the Han Dynasty have also been found at **Lingtou Monastery**, though the present building with its seven altars is merely 200 years old. It is inhabited by one monk who has to cope with severe security problems arising from the monastery's isolated position. Indeed, although it is only 15 minutes from Castle Peak Monastery, many local people do not know of its existence. So go armed with precise instructions from the HKTA.

The Taoist monastery **Ching Chung Koon** (close to Castle Peak Hospital), although of traditional design, was founded in 1949. It includes an old people's home which is funded with the help of the monastery's popular vegetarian restaurant. It has an extensive library and some priceless works of art. For those interested in bonsai there are marvellous examples everywhere.

Growing flowers for New Year Festivities

Far away at the western entrance to Hong Kong is the fishing village of **Lei Yue Mun**, traditionally the haunt of pirates and until recently only accessible by boat (still the most exciting way of getting there; a pre-dinner trip through the harbour is particularly recommended). Today it is the haunt of seafood lovers. The system of dining here involves a curious division of labour. Wander down the narrow streets edged with bubbling fish tanks and gaudy signs, bargain for the fish of your choice (a Cantonese-speaking friend will be invaluable here), then, armed with flapping plastic bags, choose a restaurant in which to have your purchases cooked and served. **Wai Lung Seafood** Restaurant is popular, always jostling with people both eating and playing mahjong. Finish off a delicious meal by stopping at a stall making fresh, paper-thin egg rolls. A blob of batter is dropped onto a sizzling pan and then deftly rolled up. The stall next to No. 41b on the playground corner is to be recommended.

A separate limb of the New Territories land mass is the extravagantly beautiful and mountainous **Sai Kung Peninsula**. Sai Kung town, half new, half old, has a typically cluttered Chinese market. Along the waterfront are several restaurants, their outside tables decked with gay table cloths. The brave can take their fish to the Sam Hoi (Three River) Restaurant, which is built on stilts over the sea. They serve delicious noodles. Before leaving visit the attractive Tin Hau temple.

Thirty square miles of the Sai Kung Peninsula are administered by the Country Park's Authority. (This government body looks after a total of 107 square miles of Hong Kong's most beautiful countryside.) In an effort to preserve its flora and fauna they employ rangers and fire crews, hill fires being a real threat during the summer months, and have erected barbeque areas and charted some adventurous walks. The longest of these is the **MacLehose Trail** which at 60 miles starts at Pak Tam Chung on the peninsula and runs the whole breadth of the New Territories, through eight Country Parks and over some of its wildest terrain. It is possible to enter the **Sai Kung Country Park** by car but you need a permit (from the Department of Agriculture and Fisheries) which takes at least a week to obtain. One can, however, leave one's car at the entrance of the restricted area within which there are frequent bus services.

Many traditional beliefs are still adhered to in these rural areas. In Long Keng near Sai Kung an ancient banyan tree is worshipped. Trees are supposed to house the soul of a god, who can prevent sickness and aid fertility. A shrine is often placed on or at the foot of the tree and, to ward off evil spirits, strips of red paper decorate it. Another important village deity is the Well God, who keeps the village water supply both topped up and pure. His shrine will often be beside the well.

One of the most picturesque features of the Sai Kung Peninsula is **Rocky Harbour**, an enormous island-strewn stretch of water carved out of its southeast flank. A trip undertaken by few visitors but well worthwhile is to explore Rocky Harbour by boat, hiring a small craft from Hebe Haven pier (the HKTA will suggest whom to contact). This opens up endless possibilities to visit sandy coves, small islands, and remote villages.

Outlying Islands

Lantau

The Hong Kong archipelago consists of 235 islands. Some of these barely qualify as they are simply blobs of rocks. However, the largest, Lantau, is twice the size of Hong Kong Island. This is a staggeringly beautiful island of mountains, mists, monasteries — it is sometimes called the Island of Prayer — peace and calm. With a predominantly mountainous terrain and little industrial development, Lantau only supports a population of some 20,000. Try and visit Lantau during the week: it becomes the property of multitudinous day trippers and campers at the weekends.

Although knowledge of Lantau's early history is sparse it is believed to have been settled since prehistoric times. In 1277 the doomed last emperor of the Sung Dynasty fled to Lantau from the New Territories. Some say a temporary court was set up in the Tung Chung valley — indeed several families claim to be direct descendants of the Sung courtiers.

Under development is a new commercial/residential resort, **Discovery Bay**, with a population of 1,700. Phase I of the development was completed at the end of 1982. Discovery Bay Golf Club and Village Resort are open to the public with a wide range of recreational facilities including a 18-hole golf course, tennis courts, swimming pool, water sports and billiard.

Ferries run from the Outlying Districts Pier in Central to **Silvermine Bay** (about one hour) on the east coast or Tai-O on the far west coast. From Silvermine Bay one can hire a car or take a bus across the island and then return on the ferry from Tai-O. Some of the Silvermine Bay ferries stop at Peng Chau. Do not disembark unless you wish to visit Lantau's **Trappist Monastery** dedicated to Our Lady of Joy. The monk's boat meets every Peng Chau ferry and for about $2 will take you across the small channel to the foot of a flight of steps leading to the monastery. Each day the monastery cows produce 1000 pints of milk and their chickens 600-700 eggs. One can walk from here to Silvermine Bay in about two hours.

At Silvermine Bay the bus terminal is just opposite the ferry exit. To hire a mini bus ring Lantau Tours (5-9848256) before leaving Hong Kong Island. There is little to see in Silvermine Bay itself (silver was mined there briefly during the last century). Along the beach are a group of good seafood restaurants: the Sampan (formerly Ned Kelly's Last Stand) and Seaview also serve western food. **Pui-O** nestling under the majestic Sunset Peak is the next village on the road. It has a selection of guesthouses and restaurants and across some meadows a long, slightly grey beach. Lantau's most beautiful beach accessible by road is at **Cheung Sha**. This lies between Pui-O and the Shek Pik reservoir.

For the walker Lantau is a paradise. But it is not difficult to get lost (or worse) on its precipitous terrain. Wear 'snake proof' shoes, take a strong stick, a good map and sensible precautions. *Selected Walks in Hong Kong* and the HKTA's leaflet *Lantau Walks* are useful companions. For a beautiful walk that is neither particularly hazardous nor too taxing turn left down Wang Pui Road just after the Shek Pik reservoir (if you are in a car you will have to leave it by the waterworks barrier), and take the path along the headland to **Fan Lau** (about three hours) where there is a ruined fort

Hakka lady in paddy field

and two small isolated beaches. From Fan Lau it is possible to hire a junk or if you feel energetic to walk the five miles round to Tai-O.

Continuing on from Shek Pik reservoir the road winds up between dense vegetation and then at the watershed opens out to display a beautiful valley with the Pearl Estuary lying beyond. The hillside on the right is dominated by two monastery buildings, Po Lin and Yin Hing, their yellow roofs shining against the dark green vegetation. There are no fewer than 135 monasteries on Lantau, the most famous and largest being **Po Lin** (Precious Lotus). It is situated 2500 feet above sea level and was first used by monks in 1905 but not inaugurated as a monastery until 1927. Its present buildings date from 1970. There are 100 resident monks and nuns who, with the help of about a hundred old people look after the monastery and manage a commercial tourist enterprise. Their vegetarian restaurant brings in roughly $50,000 per month. Two thousand tourists visit the community most weekends but it is planned to increase this by building a cable car up from the valley. On stepping out of the cable car the visitor will be greeted by a 30-foot standing Buddha. The ornate main temple is dedicated to the Three Precious Buddhas and the stone floor is inlaid with the lotus pattern. To Buddhists the lotus is the symbol of the attainability of Nivana whatever one's past: 'it grows out of mud but it is not defiled'. You can reach the monastery by bus, or on foot, spend the night there and then climb neighbouring **Lantau Peak** (3000 feet above sea level) and watch the sunrise.

A 10-minute walk from the monastery, on **Ngong Ping Plateau**, is a **tea plantation**. In 1959 a British barrister, with experience of Ceylon, noticed some disused tea terraces in the area. Today there is a 70 acre farm producing 36,000lbs of tea (both Indian and Chinese) per annum.

The road to the small town of **Tai-O** is bordered by the dry fields of old salt pans. Two hundred years ago Tai-O salt factories flourished. As a result of this connection, Tai-O remains a large producer of salt fish. The village is built half on Lantau and half on another island and connected by a charming flat-bottomed ferry pulled and poled by two old ladies (fare 50 cents). At the far end of the village on the island side stands **Hou Wang Temple**, which was built in 1699 (during the K'ang Shi Emperor's reign) and dedicated to Marquis Yang Liang Chieh, the uncle and guardian of the last Sung Emperor. Each year a festival is held in his memory: an enormous theatre is constructed in the temple's forecourt and opera is performed. The houses along the shore are curious to say the least, being constructed of upturned boats incarcerated in metal sheeting. This method is used to contrive even two-storeyed affairs complete with verandas and roof gardens. Often the house fronts are supported picturesquely on stilts in the water. Practically every other shop in the village sells its famed salt fish which hang like Italian salamis, their heads neatly packaged in paper. Tai-O has some lovely old shops including an 80-year old traditional medicine shop (some way down Wing On Street on the Lantau side). Inside an overwhelming perfume of sandal wood and herbs fills the air.

The only road to **Tung Chung** on the northern shore climbs over the central spine of Lantau, overlooked from their hillside vantage point by several monasteries and with Sunset Peak towering to the right. The remains of a 17th-century fort stand guard over Tung Chung, its six cannons having been recently restored.

Cheung Chau

Lantau's small neighbour Cheung Chau is a thriving fishing community which was for hundreds of years the haunt of pirates, traders and smugglers. Today this island with an area of one square mile has almost double the population of Lantau. Its main street buzzes with the activity of a typical market with plenty of food and drinks stalls for the hot and footsore visitor.

Try the sea food at the floating restaurant, **Cheung Chau Marriage Boat**. After wandering in the market and its side streets — there are several good jade shops where occasionally bargains can be found — visit the **Pak Tai Temple** (to the left when you get off the ferry). This is the scene of the famed Cheung Chau Bun Festival [see Festivals]. The temple built in 1783 houses an early statue of Pak Tai — the god of the north — and a Sung Dynasty sword salvaged from the sea during the last century.

By crossing the thin central strip of land it is possible to make a circular walk around the southern part of the island. The **beaches** along Peak Road (named somewhat obscurely **Tun Wan**, **Afternoon**, **Morning** and **Italian**) are all good for a cooling swim. Just beyond the Italian beach is the Cheung Po Tsai hideout cave. Although bearing the name of the infamous 18th-century pirate it is now thought unlikely that he ever visited it. From Sai Wan village either walk or take a sampan back to the ferry pier.

Peng Chau

Peng Chau is a much quieter affair. Although its 8000 inhabitants are predominantly fisherfolk, there is some cottage industry including several porcelain factories. Yuet Tong have a factory employing 100 people. Like Cheung Chau the island has no motor cars and one can wander peacefully through the narrow streets. There are noodle stalls and restaurants a-plenty. Employ the Lei Yue Mun [see New Territories] technique: buy your fish on the pier and then take your writhing bag to **Sun Kwong Restaurant** (5-9830239) for its contents to be cooked. On the way to the porcelain factories, depending on the weather, you may see tray upon tray of tiny fish drying in the sun: most likely your nose will notice it first.

Lamma

Just south of Aberdeen lies Lamma, at five square miles Hong Kong's third largest island. Fragments unearthed in Shan Wan Bay, and stone rings attributed to the Shan Yao aboriginal people, provide evidence of Lamma's prehistoric background. Today this rugged mountainous island of sparse vegetation has a population of 5000 people engaged in vegetable and fish farming and some cottage industry. It has potentially lovely beaches but unfortunately Lamma's proximity to Hong Kong Island and the main shipping lane mean that the water is often polluted.

There are two main villages on Lamma both served by ferry leaving from Hong Kong's Outlying Districts Pier. Alternatively you can take your life in your hands, hire a sampan from Aberdeen and make a dash across the paths of giant container ships into **Sok Kwu Wan**. There is little to see in the village but plenty to eat, as a whole series of outdoor restaurants lines the shore. North of here, St. George's Bay with its small Tin Hau temple and fishing community, is the scene once a year of spectacular Dragon Boat

Races [see Festivals]. To enable more crews to compete, these races are held on a separate day to the gazetted festival day. Here the traditional religious part of the festival is observed punctiliously, every team bringing their lion dancers and offerings to pay homage to Tin Hau at the temple. It is a thrilling day and if you are visiting Hong Kong in early June one not to be missed.

From Sok Kwu Wan it is a gentle two-hour walk, mostly along the coast, passing desirable (depending on the tides) **Hung Shing Ye beach** and one of Hong Kong's two enormous new power stations and finishing at

Pleasure cruise, Aberdeen

Yung Shu Wan, where you can catch a ferry back to Central. This small town also has a waterfront decorated with restaurants.

Other Islands

Two ferries a day that call at Sok Kwu Wan then go on to **Po-Toi** a group of four rocky islands. The largest Po-Toi has a delightful small village of gaily painted houses, which are slightly Mediterranean in feeling, built around a wide bay. This bay is the scene of a colourful rural festival on the birthday of goddess Tin Hau in May [see Festivals]. By clambering round the rocks from the village you will come upon some rock carvings, allegedly 3500 years old, which are thought to be Burmese or Khmer. After the exhausting scramble back, visit the restaurant on the right (looking from the sea) which serves ice-cold beer and delicious fish.

In addition to these more accessible islands the group in **Rocky Harbour** [see New Territories] is highly recommended for a visit. **Double Haven** is really too remote to be discovered by any but the luckiest or most pioneering of short-term visitors. This is a natural harbour formed by a group of islands in Mirs Bay very close to the Chinese mainland. Quite simply it offers some of the most beautiful sea and mountain scapes in the world. If you get the chance to go, take it.

Tours in Hong Kong

Local entrepreneurial talents have produced an astonishingly wide selection of tours in Hong Kong. Enthusiastic brochures encourage you to sip cocktails while travelling on a tram from Causeway Bay to Western or go on shopping expeditions with American expatriate wives, or drive up the Peak for a 'night view' and down again to Wanchai to sample a 'night spot.'

All these things (without the frills), can of course be done alone. But if you do opt for a tour, then select with caution or you many find yourself simply on a glorified shopping expedition to spots where your guide is assured of a percentage of your purchase. And be aware that touring by coach, especially in the New Territories, may simply turn out to be half a day sitting in heavy traffic staring at unsightly half-constructed new towns.

Probably most worthwhile is Hong Kong Watertours which has an impressive range of trips of different lengths, some combining sea and land touring, others simply offering relaxed drinks or meals on board while the boat sails past parts of Hong Kong's varied shoreline — more comfortable, more isolated and much more expensive than just taking the usual public ferry. Two other interesting and well organised tours are a visit to the Sung Dynasty Village [see Kowloon] and a cruise on the Hong Kong Hilton's Wan Fu — a replica of a 19th-century Royal Navy pirate chaser. Bookings can be made at your hotel.

Excursions from Hong Kong

Tours to China

Since the border between Hong Kong and Canton opened in 1978 the flow of visitors into Canton (Guangdong) Province has not ceased. The vast majority are Hong Kong Chinese visiting relatives, but the colony also acts as the main gateway into China for foreigners, and thousands of tourists and businessmen begin their China travels on a train, plane or hovercraft bound for Canton.

China Travel Service (HK) Ltd (the agent in Hong Kong for China International Travel Service who handle all aspects of foreign travel within China) offers a range of group tours lasting from 3-14 days to several different parts of China. They also offer the more pricey 'individual tour' to a few cities — a contradictory-sounding package which gives a little more freedom than the usual group tour. The most attractive longer tours tend to get booked up well in advance, but there may be cancellations for the last-minute traveller to snap up. CTS offices are at 77 Queen's Road Central (tel. 5-259121) and 27-33 Nathan Road (tel. 3-667201). Most travel agents in Hong Kong will handle the booking of CTS tours to China (for which they receive a flat commission).

An increasing number of Hong Kong's tour operators and agents are running their own tours, bypassing CTS and negotiating directly with the authorities in China. Some of these tours may be more expensive, but may also offer extra facilities which a straight CTS tour does not (an escort from the Hong Kong office, for example, to iron out all problems that inevitably greet travellers in China). It is worth checking carefully on these points before selecting your tour. Competition is of course keen in Hong Kong especially among operators and agents offering short trips (6 days in Peking, 3 in Canton, 4 or 5 days in Shanghai, for example) and cheaper tour prices may simply indicate that agents are undercutting each other.

Day trips to China

CTS offer two tours from Hong Kong — one just over the border to Shenzhen (spelt Shumchun in Hong Kong) and the other to the county of Zhongshan (Chungshan) entering China through Macau. Of the two, the trip via Macau is far superior. It takes you by hydrofoil from Hong Kong to Macau (70 minutes) where you cross the border into an attractive landscape of paddyfields and traditional Cantonese villages. A tour bus takes you to the birthplace of Dr Sun Yat-Sen (regarded by the Chinese as the founder of modern socialist China) and on to a county town for lunch. On the way back to Macau you visit a commune, fishing village or kindergarten. The

cheaper trip to Shenzhen offer less chance to see anything of Guangdong
Province. The town, with 300,000 or so inhabitants, is distinctly untypical
since it is one of China's special economic zones, established to attract
foreign (particularly Hong Kong) investment. High rise residential and
commercial blocks are under construction, industry is growing, and
accompanying social problems associated with the town's sudden economic
boom are much in evidence. A visit to the Shenzhen Reservoir, which is
one of the main suppliers of water to Hong Kong, is included in this visit.

Day trips to Macau

Few foreign visitors can resist the particular magic of this tiny colonial
outpost, founded in 1557, and consisting of only six square miles of
Portuguese territory — a small peninsula attached to the Chinese mainland,
together with two tiny green islands.

The large majority of Macau's visitors are residents of Hong Kong who
look no further than the casino — a markedly unglamorous 24-hour
gambling palace with a phenomenal turnover. But for those who ignore the
tables, Macau offers a relaxed, wistful look at the past. Unlike Hong Kong,
and despite a burst of redevelopment, there are many visual reminders of
the colony's history. Old colonial-style buildings overlook the Praia Grande;
17th century fortresses, churches, mansions still stand; traditional Chinese
shops set in colonnades thrive; and there are cobbled streets lined with two-
or three-storeyed terraced houses, the line between squalid and
picturesque being finely drawn. Some excellent Chinese food is to be had,
but even more appealing are the Portuguese restaurants which serve
wholesome country food — fish buried in a sauce of tomato and olives,
stews thick with potatoes, and colonial dishes such as African chicken and
chilli prawns all washed down with inexpensive Portuguese wine.

There is no reason to take a tour here. Simply take one of the frequent
jetfoils (around 50 minutes), hydrofoils (around 70 minutes) or ferries (2½
hours) from the Macau Ferry pier in Central. Bookings can be made up to a
week in advance — advisable at any time, and essential for weekends and
public holidays. You need your passport to enter Macau. (The Macau
Pataca is the legal currency there, but the Hong Kong dollar circulates
freely.) It is an easy place to get around in, especially after the pressures of
Hong Kong. There are plenty of taxis, buses and pedicabs, and several
guide books on the market which can direct you to the right spots.

(Following page) Aberdeen & Ap Lei Chau with floating restaurants in foreground

Restaurants

An indication of costs is given below. One star means inexpensive (below $50 per person), two stars mean moderately cheap ($50-$100), three stars for moderately expensive ($100-$150) and four stars stand for over $150 per head, not including drinks. Applied to Chinese restaurants prices are calculated per person for a party of four to six.

Chinese

美利堅飯店　灣仔駱克道23及20號
AMERICAN RESTAURANT
20 Lockhart Road, Wanchai, Hong Kong
Telephone 5-277277

This Peking restaurant doesn't feature Peking duck. Instead highly recommended for winter eating are the hot pots, the mutton with great bunches of spring onions, and sometimes lamb. The fried dumplings and steamed dumplings are both light and superb, the former very crisp, and an excellent starter in winter is the Tsientsin cabbage in a chicken oil. Other excellent dishes include fried shrimp with little garlic leaves, and a mushroom soup which is unique: the usual big Peking mushrooms are at the bottom, but floating on top is a bunch of crisp 'Peking spinach' leaves (there is no English name to this unique vegetable). Like most Chinese restaurants, it is very crowded at lunchtimes. Best bet of all is to look around at other tables and see what looks — and smells — best. Then order the same.

點心
DIM SUM
Virtually every Cantonese restaurant accompanies morning tea with *dim sum* hors d'oeuvres. And so much are they associated with tea that *yum cha* — literally, 'drink tea' automatically means tea with *dim sum*. The food isn't so much a meal as a very happy ritual of almost classical Chinese leisure: sitting, drinking that most sublime of drinks, tea, and eating a variety of dishes without ever hurrying. More and more, though, hustling, bustling Hong Kong lacks the time for such efforts. So on Sundays, the *dim sum* restaurants become chaotic scrambles for seats, and no visitor should venture in on any holiday. But on weekdays (preferably long before lunch), a *dim sum* restaurant is an ideal place for eating, relaxing and seeing a traditional way of life which hasn't yet disappeared.

While one need merely point to the basket of one's choice, here are a few of the better-known *dim sum* dishes: *Cha siu bau* (barbequed pork bun); *chun kuen* (spring roll), *fun gwor* (steamed meat dumpling), *har kau* (shrimp dumpling), *pai kwat* (steamed spare ribs) and *tsing ngau yuk* (steamed beef ball in a lotus leaf).

The prime 'historical' *dim sum* restaurant is Luk Yu Tea House (q.v.). Other well-known restaurants on Hong Kong side include the Rainbow Room in Lee Gardens Hotel; the Hopewell City Restaurant on the eighth floor of Hopewell Centre, 183 Queen's Road, Wanchai; Yung Kee, at 32 Wellington Street, Central; and Glorious, 41 Lockhart Road in Wanchai. On Kowloon side, half a dozen *dim sum* restaurants along Nathan Road are famous. These include Golden Wheel at 172 Nathan Road, the Golden Crown at 70 Nathan Road, Kingsland, in the Miramar Hotel; and Oceania in Ocean Terminal on the second floor.

楓林小館　西貢兆日樓　沙田材林道45號
FUNG LUM
a) Shiu Yat Building, Saikung Telephone 3-2816623, 3-2811348
b) 45 Tsuen Nam Road, Shatin, New Territories Telephone 0-621175

Fung Lum is a Cantonese-style chain which extends from the New Territories to California, yet still preserves its high standards. Even those not addicted to beancurd should find *one* of the 17 varieties to their liking (I plunk for roast beancurd which is mashed, sieved and steamed until lightly roasted to a delicate brown). Out of the enormous menus, the choice is such that only the largest parties won't feel they're missing something special. The smoked duck is always recommended: the preparation is a complicated process in which the duck is scalded, wind-dried, smoked over wood chips, tea and charcoal, and then steamed. Also try the sliced beef with chilli and bean sauce. Shrimp baked with salt isn't exactly Cantonese (more Hakka), but the chicken with lemon sauce can be good. It's best to caution the waiter not to make it *too* sweet. Out of 200-odd dishes, this choice is the easiest one. Instinct is usually the best policy.

Incidentally, Fung Lum also manages a restaurant in the New Territories on a hillock overlooking the habour on the Taipo Road above Shatin. Named Yucca de Lac, on Lot 716 in the village of Ma Liu Shui, it specialises in Cantonese-style seafood, has a beautiful view, and is enjoyed by foreigners and Chinese alike.

金紅潮洲酒家　尖沙咀寶勒巷13號
GOLDEN RED CHIU CHOW RESTAURANT * *
13 Prat Avenue, Tsimshatsui, Kowloon Telephone 3-666822

Chiu Chow Chinese food is hardly the favourite of visitors. Outside of the wallopping strong Iron Buddha tea (as strong as the muddiest Turkish coffee), Chiu Chow food is a bit too thick, a bit too extreme, has too much emphasis on offal and blood gravy. But those who want to try this cuisine from Swatow, can't go wrong with Golden Red. The best traditional dish here is the goose with soy sauce, with fried goose blood and vinegar and garlic on the side. Another Chiu Chow dish is the fried chicken balls, good fleshy pieces of chicken compacted into firm chunks along with deep-fried pearl leaves. The fried minced crab balls at $10 are a bargain, rich with fine crabmeat shreds and ginger. This is an adventure more than a really great restaurant . . . except for those who want to try a very particular Chinese cuisine.

大上海飯店　尖沙咀寶勒巷26號
GREAT SHANGHAI**
26-36 Prat Avenue, 1/F., Kowloon Telephone 3-668158
There are some who consider this to be the best Shanghai restaurant anywhere in the city. Certainly the restaurant doesn't stint on peppers, oils or garlic, and their seafood is as good as any in Shanghai itself. Actually Shanghai doesn't really have its own cuisine — like New York, it takes on much of the food styles of its various peoples. But with such fine fresh ingredients as Hong Kong has, Great Shanghai has an imaginative menu. Specials include chicken in wine sauce, where the bird is boiled and then cooked in Shiau Shing wine. Their braised eels with bamboo shoots are fine, as is the noisette of pork served with vegetables and covered in a heavy soy sauce. Prices are reasonable.

翠園酒樓　香港康樂大廈
JADE GARDEN**
Entertainment Building, Central Telephone 5-234071
1 Hysan Avenue, Causeway Bay Telephone 5-779332
Metropolitan Bank Building, Tsimshatsui Telephone 3-660788
53 Paterson Street, Causeway Bay Telephone 5-7902277
South China Athletic Association, Happy Valley Telephone 5-773337
Star House, Tsimshatsui Telephone 3-7226888
Swire House, Central Telephone 5-239966
Jade Garden is the favourite restaurant of a) Chinese who wish to entertain their European guests; b) Europeans who wish to entertain their guests from overseas, c) visitors from overseas, and d) residents who aren't *that* fond of Chinese food. The Jade Garden menus are all moderately appetizing, the places are clean, prices moderate, service is good . . . but what is missing is the adventure of eating Chinese food. Banquets invariably consist of the Hong Kong equivalent of sweet-and-sour nothings, usually the same corn soup, beef with almonds, barbecued pork, mushrooms and vegetables and apple fritters. The Beggar's Chicken is very good, the other dishes fresh. And nobody, but nobody ever complains about a Jade

Garden meal. At the same time, nobody remembers them very well.
Certainly Jade Garden is an improvement on London or most New York
Cantonese restaurants. But in a city brimming with such excellent cuisine,
Hong Kong's more imaginative diners usually plunk for restaurants with
more verve and more life to their food.

敬賓酒家　皇后大道中158號
KING BUN RESTAURANT · · ·
158 Queen's Road, Central, Hong Hong Telephone: 5-430300, 5-432223
　　Hong Kong's top Chinese writer on food, William Mark, figures that
King Bun may be the best Cantonese restaurant in the whole city — and he
may well be right. Certainly, I have never had a bad meal here. The
atmosphere is subdued, well-worn, unpretentious; the food fairly
inexpensive; and the dishes brilliant. With a menu of nearly 500 dishes, it's
possible to give only a small selection. First, this is the *only* restaurant
recommended for that old favourite, sweet and sour pork, which includes
green and red peppers and Chinese onion in a marvellous balance. They
also have the best pigeon outside of Lung Wah (q.v.), Yunnanese ham
casserole which is unique, barbecued duck with other meats, a lot of fine
wild animal fare for wintertime (including excellent snake soup), and all
sorts of vegetable dishes. Warning: go with a large party, choose *carefully*,
try to get the confidence of one waiter or another; and your banquet can be
supreme.

陸羽茶室　中環士丹利街24號
LUK YU RESTAURANT · ·
24 Stanley Street, Central Hong Kong Telephone 5-232973
　　If Hong Kong has better *dim sum* in a modern setting, then Luk Yu has
the most historic *dim sum*. The restaurant was originally opened in 1925,
and it still has that old feeling: black mahogany chairs, old menu scrolls on
the walls, stained glass panels, brass spittoons. It is a little difficult to order
the *dim sum*, because no English menu is available, and the dishes are not
paraded around, but with a friendly waiter at your side, you can have meat
dumplings cooked with tangerine peel, minced ham in thousand layer cake,
chicken pie, fried shrimp roll, toasted duck with rice in lily leaves — and
hundreds more. Dinners are also served here, but the menu gives little
indication of the specials. Again, ask a friendly waiter. Marvellous
atmosphere, though fearfully crowded in the morning.
　　Be warned that the morning 'regulars' are so well-known that foreigners
frequently get short shrift. So it's almost essential to go here with Chinese
friends during the daytime.

龍華酒店　新界沙田下禾輋22號
LUNG WAH HOTEL**
22 Ha Wo Che, Shatin, New Territories Telephone 0-611648

This is an astonishing restaurant if you love pigeon. With 24 different pigeon recipes on the menu (and many more off), it's no wonder that old Lung Wah serves 2000 pigeons a day — and over one-million a year. Here, you should try everything from satay pigeon to roast pigeon, baked pigeon, pigeon egg with mushroom, steamed pigeon heart, and more. The snake soup is marvellous during the cold season, and Lung Wah has a fine hot pot with glutinous rice and sausages. The restaurant's semi-outdoor, very crowded on the weekends, but relaxed during the week. Your best bet is to drive past Shatin itself on the road to Tai Po, then park the car or stop the taxi, near Kilometre 9 (you'll see the restaurant from here) and walk over the overpass, through a little aviary.

荔香村酒家　威靈頓街15D　尖沙咀金馬倫道 9 號
LYCHEE VILLAGE RESTAURANT**
15D Wellington St, Central Hong Kong Telephone 5-245744, 5-245730
9-11A Cameron Road, Tsimshatsui Telephone 3-686544, 3-685907

So chic-looking are both these Lychee Village restaurants, with their tiles and grilles and lanterns, that one believes they must be tourist traps. Hardly, not only are the prices fair, but they serve top-rate Cantonese fare. Baked salted shrimp or fried scallops are always fresh and firm. The casserole of braised brisket of beef with bean sauce is rich and sweet. Even the simplest dish, braised chicken liver is gently sauced in large pieces. All vegetables are equally exciting — and the cleanliness is incomparable. The food can be compared with the undoubted best, King Bun. One has a choice of traditional surroundings or a fairly ritzy ambience. But in both restaurants, the food is the most important part.

文華廳　文華酒店
MAN WAH***
Mandarin Hotel, 5 Connaught Road Central, Hong Kong
Telephone 5-220111

There are some who go to the Mandarin's Chinese restaurant for its decor: a combination of superb antiques and the most jumbled up chinoiserie, others, for the view, and others for its spacious setting. I always find Man Wah is best for its summer dishes, seasonal specialities found rarely in such profusion, like the mashed wintermelon (so called for its co-o-o-ling flavour) and crabmeat soup; or the sauteed sliced chicken with fresh mango (as beautiful to look at as to eat). Equally light is the minced pigeon sauteed in lettuce, the sauteed prawn with ginger and scallions. The Man Wah has a dozen-odd other summer specials — all *very* expensive, as befitting Mandarin prices, — but all prepared with loving care in a lovely setting.

北京樓　怡東商場　歷山大厦　星光行
PEKING GARDEN * *
1/F., Excelsior Shopping Arcade, Causeway Bay, Hong Kong
Telephone 5-777231
Alexandra House basement, Central, Hong Kong
Telephone 5-266456, 5-255688
Star House, Tsimshatsui, Kowloon Telephone 3-7226888, 3-7221155

There are some who consider the Peking Gardens chain *too* efficient, *too* neat, *too* much catering for the foreigner. It is elegant, neat, it does cater for foreigners, and to a degree, the service is so mechanical as to be off-putting. But if the restaurants lack the familial ambiance of Hoover, they do have the advantages of equally excellent food. With superb Peking duck and Beggar's Chicken, grilled hilsa herring and sizzling beef with spring onions, shrimp with peppers, and sharksfin soup which is virtually a stew of sharksfin. Peking Garden also has a nightly show of Peking noodle-making — the sight of which is like a grand acrobatic show and shouldn't be missed. The times vary, but are usually around 9.30pm in each of the restaurants, which are comfortable, excellent value for money, not exactly an adventure in eating, but predictably superb.

上海山王飯店　尖沙咀康和里 3 號
SANNO SHANGHAI RESTAURANT * *
3 Cornwall Avenue, Tsimshatsui, Kowloon Telephone 3-671421, 3-677988

This is one of the best — and most overlooked — Shanghai restaurants in Hong Kong. It's probably overlooked because it is so simple: clean, bright and comfortable, that's all. But Sanno has such fine cuisine that it can afford to be without decorative airs and graces. What it has is an experienced corps of waiters, fine prices (half-a-dozen people can dine marvellously for around $200), and better food. One must be careful, though, of the menu. A 'noisette pork rump in soup' isn't a soup at all, but an enormous slab of rump, skin, meat and fat, served with fine Chinese spinach stalk. On the other hand, 'crispy rice with assorted meats' is more like a soup, as broth is poured over crispy rice cakes. Other dishes are more to the point. The fried chicken ('large snap style') is a deep-fried ball of chicken meat to be dipped in salt and tomato sauce. The braised eggplant in soy cream sauce is creamy and rich, mixed with minced pork. And the ham-and-gourd soup is a perfect last dish for hot summers (to which can be added the fried apples coated with honey). Not known by many Sanno deserves to be on everybody's list . . . but perhaps it's just as well left to those willing to try the unknown.

鹿鳴春飯店　尖沙咀麼地道42號二樓
SPRING DEER RESTAURANT***
1/F., 42 Mody Road, Kowloon Telephone 3-664012

Spring Deer deserves a place here for its almost 40 years of service to those who love their Peking Duck. Some say that the duck has become a little oilier with the years, but it's usually browned nicely, carved with a minimum of meat on each slab of skin and has a rich smell. The old-timers stick with the duck. Others (including this writer) prefer the superb chicken which is steamed with chilli and sweet peppers then fried. The handmade noodles here are as good as at Peking Gardens, but one rarely sees them made. The buns are recommended. Another dish to order before the duck is the prawns cooked with sour-hot red chilli sauce — not half as spicy as it sounds. Prices are average.

新同樂魚翅酒家　廣東道25－27號海港城三期　跑馬地摩理臣山道78號
SUN TUNG LOK****
25-27 Harbor City, Canton Road, Tsimshatsui, Kowloon
Telephone 3-7220288
78 Morrison Hill Road, Happy Valley, Hong Kong Telephone 5-748261

I've had some of the best banquets of my life in Sun Tung Lok. But these have to be ordered beforehand — and they're usually prepared by special visiting chefs from China. The banquets are vastly expensive, a minimum of 12 is expected at a table, and they're held only at special times. It's best to have your hotel call the main restaurant at Pennington Street to find out if something special is on. If so, go. And never mind the expense, you're on holiday. The other way to enjoy this restaurant is to pay an equal amount of money and have the sharksfin and other exotic seafood, like the 'neck of giant clam' which is seen outside the Morrison Hill Road branch. The raw mollusc is served on a bed of lettuce with onion slices. The neck is dipped into a table-top fondue bowl with chicken stock. The abalone is equally delicious (and expensive), while the sharksfin supreme justifies its adjective. Equally tasty is the sauteed sliced duck with walnuts — soft and tender. Back to the sea, try the braised 'spice salted' cuttlefish, which is scored, crisp and melting in a gentle chilli-based sauce. For the grand finale, you may as well pay and take the braised bird's nest with pigeon eggs. Marvellous service, luxurious surroundings and very exotic food.

錦江春　置地廣場
SICHUAN GARDENS****
3rd floor, Landmark Building, Central, Hong Kong Telephone 5-214433

This is certainly the most expensive Szechuan-style restaurant in the city, where parties of four or five could be paying up to $200 *each* for the privilege of dining here. Is it worth the price? Yes and no. Part of the price is obviously due to its location in one of the highest-rent buildings in the world and no lover of food should subsidise rapacious landlords. But on the affirmative side, Sichuan Gardens is praised by all the Szechuanese as having the finest Szechuan food in Hong Kong — possibly better than even Taiwan, which had previously held the honours. Certainly Taiwan can't claim to have its own chefs 'borrowed' from Szechuan Province, the way Sichuan Gardens does. The result is pricy, but fit for gourmet of the highest order. The Szechuan Pigeon, smoked delicately, is plump and tasty. The beef is spiced to the right piquant degree. The hot-and-sour soup is neither too hot nor too sour. And the other dishes are all superb.

四川樓　銅鑼灣駱克道466號
SZE CHUEN LAU RESTAURANT * *
466 Lockhart Road, Causeway Bay, Hong Kong Telephone 5-8918795

There are possibly better Szechuan restaurants in Hong Kong, but none is as consistently good as Sze Chuen Lau. Service is always pleasant, the private rooms are ideal for banquets (my most enjoyable New Year's Eve banquet was spent here), and the prices are very reasonable. Start the meal with table-top cabbage, spicy of course, and then try the cold chicken with a chilli-sesame sauce. As a main dish, order the smoked duck, that most rigorous test for a Szechuan restaurant. Here the duck, smoked in camphorwood and tea leaves, is always juicy and tasty, the meat peeling straight off the bone. I've often be advised to order the orange beef but have never found it as interesting as the fine braised eel, or the eggplant or splendid beancurds of all kinds. I don't like to recommend making the food too mild, but the Sze Chuen Lau management is so helpful that they're always ready to soften things down for the faint heart or sensitive palate.

天香樓　尖沙咀柯士甸路18C
TIEN HEUNG LAU * * * *
18C Austin Avenue, Tsimshatsui, Kowloon Telephone 3-662414

The most expensive Chinese restaurant isn't at the Mandarin: it's in the middle of Tsimshatsui, and caters to Chinese movie stars rather than foreigners. Some say that Tien Heung Lau just shouldn't ask these prices — up to $125 per person with no effort at all. But others say that it's impossible to get Hangchow cuisine in Hong Kong at all, so Tien Heung Lau has the monopoly, and in a town whose totem philosopher is Adam Smith, it's a question of supply and demand. At these prices, it's best to plan carefully, hopefully with a Chinese-speaking friend, and order the best Hangchow seasonal specials. For example, Beggar's Chicken is *not* from Shanghai, but from Hangchow, and it tastes — and smells — better there than anywhere else. Then you should try the lightly fried white shrimp covered with Hangchow tea leaves, as subtle as a culinary Debussy prelude. (The leaves are harvested in May, so are best in early summer.) The deep-fried eel is exquisite, chunky with a fine garlic sauce. And the finale, a duck and wonton soup, is far better than its prosaic name. Literally half a duck is cooked and boiled with hundreds of wonton in a great clay cauldron. For your other dishes, it's best to take the advice of the management, but always ask the prices beforehand. Nobody would ever think of cheating a foreigner (the Chinese who eat here are far wealthier than the few foreigners who come in), but the prices are astounding. If on an expense account, don't miss it. P.S. Ask for the Tien Heung Lau *Chinese* wine list: you're liable to be very agreeably surprised.

鏞記酒家　威靈頓街32號
YUNG KEE RESTAURANT * *
Yung Kee Building 32 Wellington Street, Hong Kong Telephone 5-221624
Many years ago, Fortune Magazine labelled Yung Kee 'one of the world's ten best restaurants.' It was an exaggeration, to say the least, but Yung Kee is still highly rated among Cantonese gourmets. The menu has the usually 'conservative' 200-odd dishes on the menu, but you can't go wrong with the seasonal specials. For winter, ask for the snake soup with preserved duck, chicken and abalone. For spring, you'll achieve the ultimate traveller's one-up-manship if you can down the live fish, lightly steamed, or the braised pigeon with bean sauce. Summertime brings melon soup or braised abalone. And in autumn or winter, take the rice birds. Any season is good for the Yung Kee roast goose or scallops, and the well-known 'hundred-year egg' has a special incarnation in Yung Kee. No it's not a hundred years' old but use your imagination when eating here!

Other Asian
BENKAY JAPANESE RESTAURANT * * *
1st Basement, The Landmark Central, Hong Kong Telephone 5-213344-6
With Japanese restaurants fearfully expensive, and The Landmark building's prohibitive rents, one would expect Benkay to be out of the reach of anybody below the level of Chairman of the Board of Jardines or God Himself. Not true. Prices aren't cheap, but this restaurant, associated with Japan Air Lines, has such superior food, service and modern Japanese cooking gadgetry that it's a welcome addition. True, two or three people may pay up to $150 each, but they can also choose more innocently-priced dishes. There is *udonsuki*, a wonderful melange of two types of noodles, leeks, bamboo shoots, shrimps, clams, beancurd, spinach, Japanese mushrooms, cabbage, chicken and black mushrooms served on an enormous platter, then poured into a boiling bouillon bubbling in a stainless steel cauldron on a hot plate. It costs only around $60. Then there's the seaweed salad at less than $20, or a good portion of peeled tomato slices, asparagus stalks, shredded cabbage and two kinds of seaweed. Or try the

sashimi *table d'hote*, which at less than $50 could provide a whole meal: baby clam soup, a bowl of rice, a wooden platter of raw fish and a taro meat-loaf. The only real problem is that virtually none of the items are explained on the menu. One must either know, or watch, or ask for translations. Once things are translated, Benkay is a treat.

KOREA RESTAURANT * *

56 Electric Road, Causeway Bay, Hong Kong Telephone 5-711731

Most of the dozen-odd Korean restaurants in Hong Kong have the same type of cuisine, which is very different from that of Korea. They lack the homely fun of Korea, the five or six different *kimchee* (pickled vegetables) and the unbeatable spare ribs. But for what it's worth, Korea is typical of the best. Here they serve good beef barbecue or prawn barbecue, as well as peppers stuffed with beef and a few different *kimchees*. If you call in advance, Korea Restaurant will prepare chicken stuffed with ginseng root. The taste is kind of . . . well, *funny*. But those believing in the invigorating quality of *ginseng* will feel invigorated. Frankly, we'd recommend the ginseng tea instead — less expensive and apparently just as salubrious.

MAHARAJAH RESTAURANT * *

222 Wanchai Road, Ground Floor, Hong Kong Telephone 5-749838

This may be unfair, as Hong Kong has so many good Indian restaurants, but this newest one is possibly the most imaginative. To keep the record straight, many Europeans opt for the Ashoka (57 Wyndham Street, Central). Others prefer the fairly grotty atmosphere but fairly good Pan-Asian, at SMI (113 Hennessy Road, Wanchai). And across the harbour, one has a choice of the plush, pleasant curries of Gaylord (43 Chatham Road, Tsimshatsui) or a whole plethora of South Indian restaurants in questionable sanitary conditions in Chungking Mansions.

What makes Maharajah different is the variety of the dishes. The menu is very long, and the choice of curries, *sagwallahs* (spinach sauces), *masalas* (thicker curry sauces) and vegetarian dishes gives dinners much frustration. Nor would it be fair to single one out. But for the best bargain in Indian foods, lunchtime is the time for Maharajah. Here, for less than $30, one can fill up on a truly sumptuous buffet lunch, including a glass of wine or beer. There is a good selection of those extra-sweet but delicious Bengali sweets as well.

PERFUME RIVER VIETNAMESE RESTAURANT * *

51-53 Hennessy Road, Wanchai, Hong Kong Telephone 5-278644, 5-277985

89 Percival Street, Causeway Bay, Hong Kong Telephone 5-762240, 5-762472

A few years ago, illegal Vietnamese restaurants were the trendy thing in Hong Kong: little mom-and-pop affairs where you knocked three times and sat down in somebody's little apartment to gorge yourself. It was quite against the law, as none of the refugees had licenses for restaurants (and most weren't even in Hong Kong legally). That's all changed now, and the colony has dozens of fine Vietnamese restaurants. Perfume River may be the best of the lot, not much on decor (rather garish green and white walls with bright lighting), but fine on food, if a little heavy on prices. You could begin with a platter of crisp prawn crackers filled with spiced pieces of pork and giant prawn, alongside saucers of lemon and chillis. Then there are the sausages, weird soups (like pineapple-and-chicken) and the ever-popular barbecued shrimp on sugar cane. The eel curry is different from the fine Shanghai eel for the addition of vermicelli, and the fried frog's legs in butter and sweet and sour crab is fine, if you don't mind paying for a lot of shell. There's also a do-it-yourself satay, a good Vietnamese coffee, and countless other dishes, all rich with ginger and garlic, all explained well on the menu. P.S. If the Percival Road Perfume River is full, don't hesitate to cross over one block to Partridge Vietnamese Restaurant at 55 Lee Garden Road, which is equally good and where the service is much better.

THE SHEIKH * * *
89 Kimberley Road, Tsimshatsui, Kowloon Telephone 3-688554, 3-680073 (Open 7pm to after mid-night, closed on Sundays)

One of the two best Middle Eastern restaurants in Asia, the Sheikh does what the Security Council could never do. It brings Syrians, Iraquis, Lebanese and Israelis — as well as the Peak people of Hong Kong — together in a joyfully informal atmosphere. At times the atmosphere turns into dancing and singing and the ceremonial breaking of glasses. At other times, people just indulge in the food: splendid lamb kofta (meatballs), soft textured humus and tahina (sesame paste dishes), cold and hot dolmus (rice and meats wrapped in grape leaves), large portions of cold yoghurt soup and lemon soup, kebabs and much-too-sweet desserts which are irresistible. There are always specials on the black-board, always helpings of ouzo, arak and friendship, with a lot of backgammon boards for fanatics.

THE SPICE MARKET * *
Deck 2, Ocean Terminal, 2nd floor, Hong Kong Hotel, Tsimshatsui, Kowloon Telephone 3-676238

Visitors who want to get the full flavour of Asia need go no further than the huge Ocean Terminal Shopping centre. Here at the Spice Market, are recipes from virtually every Southeast Asian country. And while purists may object to the lack of really *hot* spices, the Spice Market in other respects tries to be as authentic as possible. Here you can have Singapore fried noodles, Filipino 'salmon' (actually a flavourful local salmon), Indian kofta curry, Malayan beef stew with pineapple (as well as tomato, onion and bell pepper chunks), curries from Thailand (not very Thai), and a wealth of happily fattening desserts. The most unusual is Gula Malacca, a Portuguese Malayan dish which is available nowhere else in Hong Kong. Incidentally, there are excellent views of the harbour for those who want pictures as well as provender.

FUKI ROBBATAYAKI RESTAURANT
10 Hysan Avenue, Causeway Bay, Hong Kong Telephone 5-7906530
B2 New World Centre, Tsimshatsui, Kowloon 3-7216506
This is the opposite of Benkay Restaurant in the Landmark (though, to be honest, the prices aren't as cheap as they might seem at first glancing at the menu, and with the dishes piling up, they can be fairly expensive). The Robbatayaki restaurants in Japan aren't often frequented by foreigners. These are 'country-style' simple places, based, supposedly, on farmer's food. There is nothing fancy here, just simple broiled fish, a bit of eel, some rice, pleasant vegetable combinations. The pure Robbatayaki restaurants in Tokyo are raucously happy places, with big cups of *saki* passed around, lots of singing and friendship. Fuki isn't quite in that category, and is a little stiff. But the tiny plates are healthy, clean and good, and the place is a favourite for Japanese and foreigners alike.

BARON'S TABLE * * *
Holiday Inn, 50 Nathan Road, Kowloon Telephone 3-693111
In the hot season Baron's Table affords a well air-conditioned retreat from the heat where you can enjoy a refreshing summer menu. In a fine looking medieval baronial dining room sample smoked salmon with melon, mango cocktail, prawn dumplings in dill sauce or Westphalian ham with palm hearts to name but a few. Winter brings the game menu to Holiday Inn: hare from the New Territories, New Zealand pheasant, quail, trout from the Black Forest ...it's all prepared with Teutonic thoroughness and can be delicious as it is filling. Just in case you're not into game, try the unique 'Deutsche Lander' a roast rack of lamb with garlic and mushrooms — pretty expensive, but pretty good.

THE BELVEDERE
Harbour View Holiday Inn, 70 Mody Road, East Tsim Sha Tsui, Kowloon Telephone 3-7215161
Freshness and light are the two words which best sum up the cuisine and decor of The Belvedere, Harbour View Holiday Inn's gourmet restaurant.
The menu features ocean-fresh seafood such as sautéed salmon with aged red wine vinegar on a bed of spinach, and steamed scallops in a chive sabayon sauce. Especially good hors d'oeuvres are breast of pigeon on spring salad and fresh crab wrapped in a crepe and served with a crayfish butter

sauce. Also recommended at the Belvedere are flambes and prime cuts of beef such as Chateaubriand for two, roast tenderloin with a fine goose liver sauce and fillet of beef stroganoff, served flaming at your table.

CHESA ***
Peninsula Hotel, Salisbury Road, Kowloon Telephone 3-666251
Hong Kong's only Swiss restaurant, Chesa has a simple Swiss country-inn atmosphere, albeit with Swiss *banker's* prices. Still, Chesa has always had a sense of Swiss meticulousness, with courteous service, and a warm friendly atmosphere missing from first-class restaurants in Hong Kong which believe that snobbery is an equivalent of style. All the favourite Swiss specials are here, from air-dried beef to barley soup, schnitzel, veal sausages and fondues plus absolutely marvellous veal sausages with an onion sauce and fondues. Of course when the Chesa makes *spaetzel*, they take nothing coarse or big in their dumplings: these are tiny and light. For dessert, it's best to put the extra calories on the *expanse* account and wade into the Vacherin glace — a positively unholy combination of chocolate filled with ice-cream on a meringue. Sinful!

GADDI'S ****
Peninsula Hotel, Salisbury Road, Kowloon Telephone 3-666251
I'm not as fond of Gaddi's as most tourists and residents who can afford it. Perhaps it's because Gaddi's specialises not only in gourmet cooking but in an almost intimidating snobbery as well, with a maitre d'hotel who greets only the most affluent-looking customers. But make no mistake about it: the food here is prepared with a gourmet touch, and the beauty of the place would do credit to any Parisian restaurant. Not a single dish is bad here. The chicken *à la Kiev* with wild rice is as superb as the steak *à la mode du patron*, with its onion-bacon-liver garnish. The poached perch *à l'aneth* with its delicate dill sauce is as tempting as the veal steak *Brillat-Savarin*, tender, smooth with a creamy mushroom sauce. The chicken breast on leeks with a Vermouth sauce is as tempting as the stuffed quail with wild rice, and the finishing sabayon, if fresh strawberries are in season, is the perfect way to end the meal. I personally prefer sacrificing *some* of the sauce and austerity for Au Trou Normand's informal simplicity . . . . but others dispute me. And no tourist who can afford the rather phenomenal prices should miss Gaddi's anyhow, as this is as much a Hong Kong institution as the Peninsula itself.

HUGO'S RESTAURANT ***
Hyatt Regency Hotel, 67 Nathan Road, Kowloon Telephone 3-662321
Named after the Bavarian Baron, Hugo Ludwig Wilhelm von Gluckenstein who was famed for his extravagance as a host by serving only the best in food and wine.

The decor is elegantly rustic and designed to provide privacy for business lunches and cosy candlelit dinners. Hugo's menu is varied to suit all tastes with some innovative dishes combining western cuisine with an eastern flavour, such as their Saffron Bouillion with Shark's Fin and Prawn Ragout with curried papaya sauce. The restaurant is also famous for its Lobster Bisque, U.S. Prime Rib of Beef, wide range of fresh seafood and for providing the very best in seasonal foods as soon as they are available on the market.

JIMMY'S KITCHEN * * *

1 Wyndham Street, Central, Hong Kong Telephone 5-265293
1/F., Kowloon Centre, 29 Ashley Road, Tsimshatsui, Kowloon
Telephone 3-684027

LANDAU'S RESTAURANT

257 Gloucester Road, Causeway Bay, Hong Kong Telephone 5-8935867, 5-8912901

As one family proudly owns these two restaurants, and as they have both been among the most dependable and best loved of all European restaurants (Jimmy's for over 50 years, Landau's for five years), I feel it no sin to put them together. Jimmy's on Hong Kong side has great daily specials — rack of lamb, roast duck, garoupa, pork — as well as brilliant opening pates, crabmeat canneloni and fine steaks. Landau's has an equally fine menu. And both have blackboards scattered around the restaurant with all sorts of specials, from gravlax to fresh oysters to pickled herring and fine pies. With a mellow atmosphere, fine service and moderate prices, both Jimmy's and Landau's are confident, warm, always dependable — and the absolute favourites of nearly everybody, including this writer.

MANDARIN GRILL * * * *

The Mandarin Hotel, 5 Connaught Road, Central Hong Kong
Telephone 5-220111

The management of the Mandarin Hotel tries very hard to push their Pierrot Restaurant on the top floor, but I have always preferred the warm elegance of the Grill, with its burnished copper, the roast beef trolley, the Cornish hen, the veal steak, the mixed grill and the sizzling steaks — very expensive, very worth-while.

MARGAUX * * * *

Shangri-la Hotel, 64 Mody Road, East Tsimshatsui, Kowloon
Telephone 3-7212111 Open 12 noon-3pm; 7-11.30pm

One doesn't have to savour a single bite from the Margaux menu to savour the elegance of the place. Designed by Don Ashton, the restaurant is sizable enough, but so artfully has it been designed, with its wine racks and large columns dividing the room, that one feels an intimacy even when the restaurant is packed. (Which is frequent, and reservations are highly recommended.)

This is one of seven restaurants in the deluxe Shangri-la, but it's the pride and joy of the management, with prices to match. The name, Margaux, gives the game away, that this is French through and through. But the tastes are delicately French. Though the menu only skirts *nouvelle cuisine*, the sauces are light and delicate, and the preparations are finely crafted. Lunches and dinners have different menus, but one has no hesitation in recommending for either meal the scrambled eggs on a thin crepe with a heavy piquant topping of morels, or, if in season, the fillet of salmon with an excellent wine sauce. There are always specials recommended by the head waiter, and one should ask for the crayfish, the smallest and tastiest around, with a light dill sauce. Naturally Margaux has the usual entrees of beef (from America), veal (from Holland) and garoupa (from Hong Kong), along with a well-recommended bouillabaisse.

Does one have room for dessert after all this? We forced ourselves to order the orange cream with blueberries and chopped almond and found it the cooling antidote for a hot muggy rainy Hong Kong day outside.

THE PIERROT ° ° ° °
Mandarin Hotel, 5 Connaught Road, Hong Kong Telephone 5-220111

Everything of Pierrot smacks of quiet elegance, except for the prices, which breathe loudly of opulence. The dishes, though, smack of *nouvelle cuisine*, in apposition to the heavily meaty Mandarin Grill downstairs. Here, all is light: a glazed green pea soup, or better, a subtle crabmeat soup lightly creamed, cooked, almost Cantonese style, so that every taste is natural. The salmon has a thin sauce and a sprinkling of black truffles, the lamb fillet has fresh basil, the veal cutlet comes on an artichoke heart . . . . all is done to perfection here, and the Belgian chef obviously has all the right ingredients for a successful restaurant.

RIGOLETTO ITALIAN RESTAURANT ° ° °
Ground floor, East Town Building, 14-16 Fenwick Street, Wanchai, Hong Kong Telephone 5-277144

If you want Italian food in Hong Kong, Rigoletto is a place to try. It was the only place for an Italian President, who dropped in (honestly!) and ordered (with apparent pleasure) the Parma ham and melon, the spaghetti in olive oil, garlic and red peppers, the scampi and the cherries jubilee. Others just enjoy sitting by the window, sipping their Chianti and watching the Wanchai world go by. Other people enjoy the opera music (which is sometimes, not always, on the tape recorder), and everybody enjoys Mr. Ugo, the marvellous owner-maitre d'hotel. Here are plenty of real dishes, (the saltimbocca is especially recommended), many spaghettis, and a perfect grilled liver and onions. Rigoletto is good service, beautiful decor and very Italian. (NOTE: Those who want their American-style Italian food can't go wrong with either of the five Spaghetti House Restaurants. On

Kowloon side: 3B Cameron Road; Barton Court, Harbour City,
Tsimshatsui. On Hong Kong side: 5B Sharp Street East; 85B Hennessy
Road. New Territories: Level 1, New Town Plaza, Shatin.)

STANLEYS RESTAURANT***

52 Stanley Main Street, Stanley, Hong Kong Telephone 5-938955,
5-938198

Stanley, which has the honour of being one of the very few settlements
on Hong Kong before the British arrived in 1842, never had a Western
restaurant until recently. It does have a fine beach, a fabulous market
(especially for rattan), and a happy-go-lucky atmosphere. Now, with
Stanleys Restaurant, they have good food too. The restaurant looks like a
private home (which it once was), and the European hosts make certain
that the community feels at home. The food, too, tastes home-cooked. The
menu is rather unusual: a cod's roe pate (superb), a game pie (crisp, with
pungent spiced venison), stuffed squid (filled with rice, mint, garlic and
parsley) oxtails with claret and pigeon. For dessert, there is chocolate
mousse and apple strudel with ice cream . . . amongst other dishes. Prices
are fairly expensive, and the restaurant is open only at night (except for
weekend lunches). But what a pleasant way to spend an evening . . . with
an easy bus ride back to Central, watching the lights of Hong Kong from
the most sublime vistas.

THE STEAKHOUSE***

Regent Hotel, 18 Salisbury Road, Kowloon Telephone 3-7211211

The Regent chain has always been in the forefront of interesting
restaurants, and the Hong Kong Regent is no exception. The Steakhouse is
an all-American treat: American charcoal grilled steaks (nine choices), all-
American salad buffets (about 20 ingredients of the freshest kind), even-
American deserts, like grasshopper pie and pumpkin pie, plus the best
selection of Californian wines that you'll find in Asia. It's very tasty, filling,
and the salad buffet is an innovative treat for weight-watchers. What a
shame that one must order the steak in order to qualify for the salad. The
view across the water is just as fascinating as the food, and the Regent
service is of course impeccable.

The Regent also has a Continental restaurant, Plume. Among its
22 specially created dishes are a spring salad with crab pincers, mushrooms,
chives and herbs; a soup of artichoke hearts and Beluga caviar; fillet of sole
and garoupa in champagne sauce; and quail breasts sauteed in hazelnut
butter with broccoli and Muscat grapes. (If you have to ask the price you
can't afford it!)

Hotels

Hong Kong has some of the best hotels in Asia, and perhaps the world, in terms of comfortable, well-equipped guest rooms, efficient and friendly service, imaginative decor, marvellous views and top notch facilities for wining, dining, meeting and relaxing.

At the end of 1984, there were approximately 18,000 hotel rooms in Hong Kong, more than 12,000 of which were classified by the Hong Kong Tourist Association as deluxe or first class.

Whichever hotel you choose in the top categories, it is likely to be a modern high-rise building with air-conditioned rooms which include private bathroom, telephone, colour television and often a refrigerator and mini-bar. The odds are that the views will be spectacular. Keen competition keeps the standard of service very high and most hotels have round-the-clock room service.

Hotels in the moderately priced category are clean, comfortable and efficiently staffed. They tend to be alittle farther from the tourist hubs but are well served by taxis and public transport.

All hotels have good restaurants. The smaller ones might have one dining room, serving European and Chinese food. The large hotels contain some of the best restaurants in town [see Restaurant List], and much local entertaining takes place here.

The hotels are also used extensively for business meetings, conferences, art exhibitions, trade promotions and special events such as antique auctions.

The following list offers a brief description of Hong Kong's hotels. All add 10% service and 5% tax to the bill. Listing in alphabetic order. Rates are in Hong Kong dollars.

Golf at Fan Ling

Hotel List

Hotel	Description	Facilities
Central District		
Furama InterContinental 1 Connaught Rd. tel. 5-255111	An elegant high-rise with 571 rooms beside the harbour, close to ferry and MTR. It has busy meeting areas and a spectacular revolving restaurant. Rates $820-920 double.	4 restaurants, 2 bars, revolving restaurant, disco
Hilton 2A Queen's Rd. tel. 5-233111	Centrally located with 821 rooms, popular restaurants and superb pool terrace. It has regular dinner-theatre presentations. Rates $830 double.	4 restaurants, 6 bars pool, Brigantine cruises, Business Centre
Mandarin 5 Connaught Rd. tel. 5-220111	In easy reach of Central offices, a hub of local and visiting businessmen. Famed for service, restaurants and Roman-bath. It has 565 rooms at $1065-1480 double.	5 restaurants, 3 bars health club & pool, Business Centre
Victoria Connaught Rd. Central tel. 5-407228	The new hotel in Hong Kong's Central district boasts spectacular harbour views for 75% of it's 540 rooms and 330 apartments. $600-950 double.	3 restaurants, lobby lounge, music room, pool, health club and business centre
Causeway Bay		
Caravelle 84-86 Morrison Hill Rd. Happy Valley tel. 5-754455	Opposite the race course, a convenient, comfortable and moderately priced hotel, 94 rooms at $440 double.	Bar, restaurant, coffee shop
Excelsior 281 Gloucester Rd. tel. 5-767365	Next to the cross-harbour tunnel and close to shops, restaurants and nightlife. Famous for its nightclub and sports facilities. Its 958 rooms are $750-1150 double.	3 restaurants, 3 bars, nightclub, tennis courts, health club
Harbour 116 Gloucester Rd. Wanchai tel. 5-748211	On the waterfront, close to nightclubs, restaurants, a friendly and reasonably priced hotel with 187 rooms at $330-420 double.	Nightclub, bar, 2 restaurants
Hong Kong Cathay 17 Tung Lo Wan Rd. tel. 5-778211	In Causeway Bay, a quiet, comfortable hotel with 142 rooms, moderately priced at $350-390 double.	Restaurant, coffee shop
Lee Gardens Hysan Avenue tel. 5-767211	Close to the nightlife and shops of Causeway Bay, the hotel has large public areas and 809 rooms at $630-850 double.	3 restaurant, 3 bars
Luk Kwok 67 Gloucester Rd. Wanchai tel. 5-270721	On the Wanchai waterfront and reputed to be the haunt of "Suzie Wong", this is a comfortable and respectable 102-room hotel. Rates are $290-340 double.	Nightclub, 4 restaurants
Park Lane 310 Gloucester Rd. tel. 5-7901021	Opposite Victoria Park and close to busy Causeway Bay. Its 850 rooms are $550-1200 double.	4 restaurants, disco, sauna, massage

Singapore
41 Hennessy Rd.
tel. 5-272721

A hotel with 165 rooms in the heart of Wanchai with good food and atmosphere. Rates are $330-360 double.

2 restaurants, bar

Kowloon

Ambassador
Nathan/Middle Rd.
tel. 3-666321

At the head of Nathan Road, close to shops and nightclubs, a friendly hotel with 320 rooms, $520-780 double.

3 restaurants, bar, nightclub

Astor
11 Carnarvon Rd.
tel. 3-667261

In the heart of Tsimshatsui's nightlife and shopping, a hotel which is comfortable and reasonably priced with 150 rooms at $380 double.

2 restaurants, bar

Empress
17 Chatham Rd.
tel. 3-660211

Convenient to downtown Kowloon and the airport with 188 rooms. Rates are $530-690 double.

2 restaurants

Fortuna
355 Nathan Rd.
tel. 3-851011

In busy Mongkok area, catering to Southeast Asian groups with 193 rooms, good food and rates of $390-420 double.

3 restaurants, Business Centre

Grand
14 Carnarvon Rd.
tel. 3-669331

In the centre of the entertainment area, a good reliable hotel with 194 rooms at $550-650 double.

2 restaurants, bar

Holiday Inn Golden Mile
50 Nathan Rd.
tel. 3-693111

On the shoppers' 'gold mile', a superbly run hotel with good bars and restaurants and 599 rooms at $700-900 double.

3 restaurants, bars, Business Centre, pool, sauna

Holiday Inn Harbour View
70 Mody Road,
tel. 3-7215161

New in East Kowloon, with good views of the harbour, the hotel has first class food and 600 rooms at $780-1080 double.

3 restaurants, bar, pool, health club, Business Centre

Hong Kong
3 Canton Rd.
tel. 3-676011

A favourite with business visitors next to the Ocean Terminal and Star Ferry, the hotel has superior food and 790 rooms at $690-1100 double.

3 restaurant, 4 bars, pool, health club

Hyatt Regency
67 Nathan Rd.
tel. 3-662321

Lively and efficient, a hotel close to the Kowloon action, known for Hugo's restaurant, it has 763 rooms at $680 double.

3 restaurants, 3 bars, night club, Business Centre

International
33 Cameron Rd.
tel. 3-663381

Convenient and comfortable, a hotel long known for moderate prices, it has 91 rooms at $400-540 double.

restaurant, bar

Kowloon
19-21 Nathan Rd.
tel. 3-698698

Opening in January 1986, and part of the Peninsula Group of hotels. It has 740 rooms at $480-980 double.

Bar, coffee shop, Business Centre

Marco Polo
Harbour City
Canton Rd.

A member of the Peninsula Group, with 441 rooms at $710 double.

3 restaurants, bar, pool, health centre, sports centre

Miramar
134 Nathan Rd.
tel. 3-681111

A city within a city, a hotel with three wings and numerous facilities, the hotel has 1198 rooms at $640-840 double.

11 restaurants, 5 bars theatre supperclub, Business Centre, Convention Centre.

Nathan
378 Nathan Rd.
tel. 3-885141

An unpretentious hotel at the top of the 'golden mile', the hotel is convenient and inexpensive with 122 rooms at $350-420 double.

restaurant, bar

New World
New World Centre
22 Salisbury Rd.
tel. 3-694111

On the edge of Kowloon bay next to a vast new shopping and entertainment complex, the hotel has 735 rooms at $450-830 double and good public facilities.

3 restaurants, bar, pool

Park
61 Chatham Rd.
tel. 3-661371

An old favourite for its large rooms and comfortable bar-lounge, the hotel is well located. It has 450 rooms at $460-650 double.

2 restaurants bar

Peninsula
Salisbury Rd.
tel. 3-666251

The *grande dame* of Hong Kong hotels with its famous lobby and fabled restaurants, the Pen has 210 rooms at $1000-3500 double.

3 restaurants, bar, lobby lounge, Business Centre

Prince
Tsimshatsui
tel. 3-7237788

Next to major shopping centres, the recently opened Prince has 402 rooms at $600-800 double.

Lobby lounge, 2 restaurants, bar and Business Centre.

Regal Meridien
East Tsimshatsui
tel. 3-7221818

A member of the Air France-Meridien chain, this 601-room hotel has 586 rooms at $750-950 double.

3 restaurants, 2 bars 1 Chinese restaurant, lobby lounge

Regal Meridien
Kai Tai Airport
tel. 3-7180333

Hong Kong's first airport hotel has 379 rooms at $300-370 double.

3 restaurants, bar

Regent
Salisbury Rd.
tel. 3-7211211

A hotel with royal box views of the harbour, a breathtaking lobby lounge, superb restaurants and 605 rooms at $930-1180 double.

5 restaurants, bars, lobby lounge, pool, health club, Business Centre

Royal Garden
East Tsimshatsui
tel. 3-7215215

A member of the Mandarin International group, it features a huge garden atrium lobby With 428 rooms, rates are $770-870 double.

Rooms overlook indoor garden

Shamrock
223 Nathan Rd.
tel. 3-662271

For budget travellers, this hotel is comfortable and convenient, with 150 rooms at $300 double.

2 restaurants, bar

Shangri-La
East Tsimshatsui
tel. 3-7212111

A deluxe hotel managed by Westin, it has fabulous decor, a fine French restaurant and 719 rooms at $800-1400 double.

4 restaurants, bar, lobby lounge, pool, sauna, Business Centre

Sheraton
20 Nathan Rd.
tel. 3-691111

Overlooking the harbour and at the head of the 'gold mile', the hotel is noted for its business facilities and international cabarets. It has 922 rooms at $900-1150 double.

5 restaurants, disco, nightclub, 8 bars, pool, Business Centre

N.B. Prices are subject to change without notice.

Recommended Reading

There is a wealth of literature and information published about Hong Kong. For authoritative historical background, Maurice Collis' *Foreign Mud* (Faber & Faber, 1964) and G.B. Endacott's *A History of Hong Kong* (Oxford University Press, 1973) are excellent.

Hong Kong's strange genesis and stranger survival is described in *Borrowed Place, Borrowed Time* by Richard Hughes (Andre Deutsch, 1968). Hughes is a veteran reporter who has lived in Hong Kong for almost 30 years and offers an intriguing and highly readable account of the place.

Austin Coates is one of Hong Kong's leading historians with a lucid and attractive style. Among his books are *Myself a Mandarin* (Frederick Muller, 1968; Heinemann (Asia) 1975) which describes his years as a magistrate, and *Whampoa* (South China Morning Post 1980) the history of local shipping.

For history, anecdote and some magnificent photographs, try *Hong Kong: The Cultured Pearl* by Nigel Cameron (Oxford University Press, 1978) and for some fascinating insights into the traditional life of rural China, Hugh Baker's two-volume *Ancestral Images* (South China Morning Post, 1979) is a winner.

The Hong Kong Government has published many excellent books dealing with different aspects of the territory. Of special note are *This is Hong Kong: Temples* (1977) with detailed descriptions of 12 Chinese temples, and *Rural Architecture of Hong Kong*, which illustrates in words and pictures some of the ancient buildings still surviving in the New Territories.

For an indispensable reference, the government publishes an Annual Review, packed with statistics, analysis and superb picture essays on just about every aspect of Hong Kong — all official, positive and reliable.

James Clavell has fictionalized the leading characters and machinations of the great *hongs*, or trading companies in *Taipan* (Dell, 1966) and *Noble House* (Hodder & Stoughton, 1981). In both books the research done was exhaustive but the facts have not been allowed to spoil a good adventure story.

The same applies to two other recent books with a Hong Kong setting. John Le Carré's *The Honourable Schoolboy* (Hodder and Stoughton, 1977) is a spy thriller featuring some recognizable local residents. Robert Elegant's *Dynasty* (Collins, 1977) is an exciting and highly fanciful saga of a Eurasian family *very* loosely based on a local clan.

Index of Places